Franz Hartman

The Life of Jehoshua - the Prophet of Nazareth

An occult study and a key to the Bible - Containing the history of an initiate

Franz Hartman

The Life of Jehoshua - the Prophet of Nazareth
An occult study and a key to the Bible - Containing the history of an initiate

ISBN/EAN: 9783337255305

Printed in Europe, USA, Canada, Australia, Japan

Cover: Foto ©Lupo / pixelio.de

More available books at **www.hansebooks.com**

THE
LIFE OF JEHOSHUA,

THE PROPHET OF NAZARETH.

An Occult Study and a Key to the Bible.

CONTAINING THE HISTORY OF AN INITIATE.

BY

FRANZ HARTMANN, M.D.,

Author of "Magic," "Paracelsus," "Secret Symbols of the Rosicrucians," Etc.

𝔄waken!

BOSTON:
OCCULT PUBLISHING COMPANY,
120 TREMONT STREET.
1888.

TYPOGRAPHY BY J. S. CUSHING & CO., BOSTON.

PREFACE.

THE only object of the following pages is to aid in dispelling the mists which for many centuries have been gathering around the person of the supposed founder of Christianity, and which have prevented mankind from obtaining a clear view of the true Redeemer, who is not to be found in history nor in external forms, but who can only be found within the interior temple of the soul by him in whom his presence becomes manifest.

It must be left to the intelligent reader to decide whether the accounts given in this book may be accepted literally as historical facts, or whether they are intended to represent eternal and ever-occurring processes going on within the inner consciousness of man. The only key to the understanding of the truth is the power to perceive it; for the truth teaches itself, — not by the light of argumentation, — but by its own light, and it teaches nothing else but itself.

All that the reading of books can possibly accomplish, is to aid us in bringing the truth which exists within ourselves to our own understanding, and to drive away the clouds of erroneous conceptions which may keep us from knowing ourselves.

There is nothing to prevent man from rising into the higher regions of thought where the light of the truth exists, except his clinging to erroneous opinions; there is no way of driving away the darkness except by the diffusion of light.

THE AUTHOR.

CONTENTS.

	PAGE
DEDICATION	7
INTRODUCTION	9
THE TRUE HISTORY OF CHRIST (*An Allegory*)	25
JEHOVAH	29
NAZARETH	38
EGYPT	48
THE MYSTERIOUS BROTHERHOOD	59
THE MYSTERIOUS BROTHERHOOD, *continued*	73
THE HIGHER DEGREES	82
THE WISDOM-RELIGION	89
THE TEMPTATION	94
THE SERMON UPON THE MOUNT	106
THE DOCTRINES OF THE CHRIST SPIRIT	118
HERODIAS	125
JERUSALEM	135
THE GREAT RENUNCIATION	145
THE TEMPLE	157
THE HERO	166
THE FINAL INITIATION	180
THE CHURCH	186
CONCLUSION	197

DEDICATION.

Eternal One! Thou self-existent Cause
Of all existence, source of love and light;
Thou universal uncreated God,
In whom all things exist and have their being,
Who lives in all things and all things in Him;
Infinite art Thou, inconceivable
Beyond the grasp of finite intellect;
Unknowable to all except thyself.
Nothing exists but Thou, and there is nothing
In which no Good exists; Thou art, but we
Appear to be; for forms are empty nothings,
If not inhabited by Thee; they are
Thyself made manifest. Addressing Thee
We sin, because we separate ourselves
In thought from Thee who art our very self;
For *we* are nothing if we are not "Thou,"
And Thou art "we"; we have no life but Thine,
No will or thought, no love or strength but Thine;
Thou art our life, our will, our mind, our all;
We are in Thee and Thou in us; Thou art
The "Father" and Thyself in us the "Son."
Thy Spirit fills the universe with glory
And impregnates all Nature with thy power,
Enabling her to bring forth living forms
Of plants and trees, of animals and men;
It fructifies the soul of man and gives
Birth to the "Christ," the saviour of man,

Call'd the divine Atma or the "Lord on high,"
The "Master," He who makes immortal all
In whom His presence is made manifest.
If He awakens in the heart of man
To the self-consciousness of His existence,
Then will there be no further death, for He
Is perfect and requires no further change.
Thus "Christ" is God made manifest in Man
As man, and no one can attain to God
Except through Him; for He Himself is God
In Man, and He who strives to find His God
Must seek for Him in His own holy temple
Within himself in Spirit and in Truth.
To Him, the Christ, the God in man we pray;
To Him alone, not to external gods,
Nor to the spirits in the Astral Light;
And praying strongly we fulfil our prayers.
For rising up to Him we are Himself,
And grant that which we ask of Him ourselves.
No man knows God; it is the God in Man
Who knows Himself in him and lifts man up
To the conception of what is divine
In his own nature. Rising up to Him
We come to God through Christ, through God to Man,
And to all nature in His Holy Spirit.

INTRODUCTION.

EVER since the beginning of the Christian era a storm of varied opinions in regard to the supposed founder of what is called "Christianity" has been raging in the world of mind, finding its expression on the external plane in deeds of violence, in innumerable cruelties, wars, atrocities, and crimes, such as are almost beyond the power of human imagination to conceive. From the time of the maniac-emperors, when the Roman arenas were reddened by the blood of the *Nazarenes*, down to the Middle Ages, when Christians had ceased to be persecuted and became persecutors in their turn ; when the scum of all Europe pillaged and plundered the inhabitants of the "Holy Land" in the assumed name of Christ ; — down to comparatively modern times, when the skies of all European countries were blackened by the smoke ascending from burning fagots, upon which men, women, and children, suspected of heresy, were roasted to death by those who claimed to be the followers of Him who had taught the doctrine of universal fraternal love ; — and still further down to our present time, in which the churches struggle to regain their waning powers and wealth, — the cause of all religious warfare has always been a difference of opinion in regard to the nature of "Christ."

While the most fanatical adherents of orthodox theology, entirely ignoring the religious histories of the world, with its *Manus*, *Avatars*, *Buddhas*, and Saviours of mankind, such as are said to have appeared upon this globe millions of years before the advent of modern "Christianity," regard the *person* of him who is called *The Christ* as being the "only begotten son" of an extracosmic creator of the world, conceived in some miraculous manner by a virgin of Palestine, and while they thus apply the most gross and sensual exoteric explanation to a beautiful ancient myth, which hides a sublime and eternal truth; the modern critic either denies that such a person as the Jesus of Nazareth of the Gospels ever existed, or he sees in him merely a man of extraordinary talents, a hero who dared to proclaim what seemed to him to be the truth; a religious reformer, who died like many others for the promulgation of a grand but impracticable idea.

Some of these critics are very profound thinkers; but they have evidently not looked behind the veil that divides the eternal, ideal, but nevertheless real world from the sensual world of illusions, wherein we live. They were unacquainted with the constitution of the "spiritual" organism of Man, and they could only see the mortal part of Jehoshua; while their opinions in regard to his spiritual nature were based upon speculations which may have approached the truth in proportion as they followed their highest intuitions.

Thus Kant regarded him as the ideal of human perfection; John Stuart Mill, as a very extraordinary man; Lord Amberly, as an "iconoclastic idealist"; Fichte, as the first teacher who revealed the unity of Man with the Supreme Spirit; Hegel, as an incarnation of the *Logos;* Schelling, as a kind of *Avatar, i.e.* one of the periodical descents of Divinity; Dr. Keim, as a mysterious man, whose glorified spirit inspired his disciples to attempt the reformation of the world; Strauss looks upon him as a moral reformer, who occasionally stooped to imposture to secure the confidence of his adherents; Renan, as an effeminate idealist, an impostor who performed "bogus phenomena"; Schleiermacher, as a man in whom self-consciousness was so saturated with the Divine principle, that he really became a god incarnate; Anatole Bembe, as a modern anarchist and socialist of the most fiery kind; and Gerald Massey, who bases his opinions upon historical researches, finds that *Jehoshua Ben-Pandira* was born some 120 years before the Christian era, and that the typical *Christ* of the gospels was made up from the features of various gods.

It appears that those who have attempted to disprove the existence of an historical personal saviour of mankind, have done no serious harm to the interest of religion; because the pious mind intuitively feels that the gospel accounts, attributed to the four Evangelists, contain after all a great deal of truth, even if the events which are told therein have never occurred in history; but those who attempt to base the whole foundation of their religious conviction upon the existence of an historical Jesus and ask others to do likewise, may be doing serious harm; for the belief in an historical Jesus can after all be merely a matter of opinion, and a faith based merely upon a possibly fallacious opinion, having no knowledge for its foundation, rests upon a very insecure basis indeed. There are very many well-meaning people upon this earth who imagine that it is indispensably necessary for one's salvation to believe that a man called Jesus of Nazareth once lived and died in Palestine; but it would be difficult to give any intelligible reason why the belief in such an historical person should be necessary for that purpose, or in what way such a belief should differ in its results from a belief in Julius Cæsar, Aristoteles, or any other person in history; as all opinions in regard to things of which we have no personal experience are merely opinions and constitute no real knowledge. To believe in an event of which we know nothing is to cling to a superstition, even if the event is actually true. We can have no self-knowledge about persons that existed before we were born; but we may at any time and at every place realize the presence of the true saviour, the eternal living Christ within ourselves.

All attempts to explain intellectually the miracles and deeds attributed to the great Nazarene, for the purpose of making it more plausible, that they have actually occurred in a literal sense, are therefore degrading to religion, and may be looked upon as a sacrilege; for they drag spiritual truths down to gross material life; they force sublime ideas into narrow material forms, and destroy the beauty of the ideal by causing it to appear in a vulgar sensual shape. Even the most exalted virtues with which a poet may endow a personal saviour will never give him that lustre which shines around the head of the eternal and impersonal Christ, and all attempts to make the beautiful allegories of the Bible agree with historical facts will be unsuccessful, and even appear ludicrous to the unprejudiced and clear-thinking observer.[1]

The question, whether or not the doctrines of the Bible are true, cannot be decided by answering the question, whether or not the events described therein have actually occurred in external life; that proof must be sought in the internal evidence of those doctrines, and this evidence will appear plain enough as soon as they are understood.

The vain attempts to prove rationally the possibility of the occurrence of miracles such as are described in

---

[1] *Gerald Massey* says: "The worst foes of the truth have ever been, and still are, the rationalizers of the myths, such as the Unitarians. They have assumed the human history [of Christ] as the starting-point and accepted the existence of a personal founder of Christianity as the one initial and fundamental fact. They have done their best to harmonize the divinity of the mythos by discharging the supernatural and miraculous element, in order that the narrative may be accepted as history. Thus they have lost the battle from the beginning by fighting it on the wrong ground." — GERALD MASSEY, *The Historical Jesus and Mythical Christ.*

the Bible, are equally absurd; for the indisputable proof that one single miracle had actually occurred, would immediately overthrow the foundation of all religions and destroy the belief in an eternal and unchanging God. God, being himself the Law, or the Cause of the Law, cannot act against himself without committing suicide, and those who are trying to uphold a belief in the possibility of anti-natural or absolutely supernatural occurrences, are denying that God is the ruler of Nature. They degrade him to a fallible being who changes his mind, and is subject to whims, such as are produced by external influences; but what external influences could possibly act upon God, who is self-existent and omnipresent and who includes the All? The fact that no miracle has ever occurred is the most formidable argument for the existence of a universal God; for it proves the existence of universal and unchangeable Law, whose Law-giver must be equally universal and not subject to change. Those, however, who attempt to reconcile the miracles of the Bible with material reason, by seeking to explain them by theories of sleight of hand, or by the spiritistic theory, are to be pitied most; for they prove that they have neither the faith which characterizes the Christian, nor sufficient intellect to see where the so-called "realities" end, and where the realm of the fable representing the true Ideal begins.

From "profane history" we can gather very little information in regard to the person of the great reformer. All that we can learn from a few short remarks in *Taci-*

tus and *Josephus* (believed by some to be interpolations) is, that some such person actually existed, and we are led to infer, that he was regarded by some as a sorcerer, by others as one of the would-be reformers and religious fanatics of those times, that he was opposed to the prevailing religious views, and that on account of the attacks he made upon time-honored institutions, upon which the security of the church and the authority of the clergy rested, he was finally put to death.

So-called "sacred history," as contained in the "four gospels," is believed to give a detailed account of his life and his doctrines; but while there seems to be a vein of truth in regard to actual historical occurrences underlying the gospel accounts, the great bulk of the latter is in contradiction to Common Sense, and merely a repetition of different allegories, such as we may find in the ancient books of the Egyptians, Persians, and Brahmins. These ancient myths have been most curiously mixed up with the biography of Jesus of Nazareth and represented as having actually taken place during his life. In fact, the few probable details in regard to the life of Jesus are so much loaded with fables and misinterpreted allegories, that the "New Testament" deserves to be regarded rather as a poem, describing psychological processes, than as a book of history, describing external occurrences.

If we examine that book without any prejudice and without any sectarian bias, we find therein two currents of thought. The first applies to the life of a man, who

—if he has not been entirely misrepresented—must have been a great genius, a hero, and a reformer. The second current refers to sacred truths, such as were taught in the secret doctrines of the Arians and Egyptians; truths which we find stated in the books of *Hermes Trismegistus*, in the *Bhagavad Gita*, and others. In these ancient books we find reference made to the *Christ principle* long before the name of "Christianity" was known, and the myths of the "Immaculate Conception," the "Son of God," etc., may be clearly traced to this ancient origin. This discovery, far from throwing discredit upon the veracity of the principles upon which primitive Christianity was based, serves rather to strengthen the foundation upon which the original doctrines rest; it does not overthrow the truths stated in the Bible, but goes to confirm them, by showing that the processes thus allegorically described, are not merely events of the past, but that they are continually occurring, and will in all probability continue to occur in the future.

It is usually claimed by those who adhere to a belief in a merely personal and historical Christ, that the gospels were written by the apostles, who having been disciples of Jesus and eye-witnesses of the miracles he performed, knew what they were talking about. Granting —for argument's sake—that these men had left some written accounts; they cannot be held responsible for all the additions and interpolations which were afterwards made by their followers and which cannot stand the test of sound reason and logic. It has however been proved by recent researches, that neither of the four gospels in their present shape was written by the apostles; but that they were probably collected long afterwards by some unknown members of the church, who labelled them with the names of the apostles, so as to impress upon them the stamp of unquestioned authority; while they undoubtedly eliminated from the existing traditions a great deal that may have appeared prejudicial to the interests of the church, or contrary to their own views and opinions.

It is not our intention to enter into a discussion in regard to the origin of the gospels, nor would we expect any great benefit to arise from a controversy in regard to such matters; because in matters of religion and where no knowledge exists, sentiment forms a stronger attraction than reason. /No argument is strong enough to force a person to lose his hold of a favorite opinion to which he has resolved to cling; while those whose knowledge is the result of mere argumentation, have usually very little power of spiritually perceiving the truth. / Those who cling to time-honored superstitions as well as those who love scepticism and sophistry, will live on the food they have chosen, until they are satiated with it. /

What does it matter to us, after all, to know whether or not our ideal Christ has ever existed in history? If we were in a position, or if it were necessary for us to imitate the daily deeds of the man Jesus of Nazareth in all their details, then would it perhaps be important to know whether or not the accounts told of these deeds are literally true; but as we are living in a different age and under different circumstances, we cannot imitate his external life in all its details; but we can look up to him as a high ideal and imitate his *inner* life, and we may live up to such an ideal without knowing whether or not it has ever been embodied upon this earth. To imitate his thoughts is far more important than imitating his personal acts.

If we look at the image of Jehoshua, seen through the trembling mists of incense, mixed with the vapors of human blood and the smoke of burning heretics, we see merely an unnatural and distorted image of the Jewish Jehovah, a ghastly-looking shadow that seems to be neither a god nor a man. If we look at him from a rational standpoint, and apply to him the rule by which mortals are usually measured, we find that our measure is somewhat too short, for we discover in him a sublimity of character, an unlimited love, a transcendental intelligence, such as is not found combined in one person in the modern history of the world; but if we look at him as being one of the full-grown flowers of humanity, a person whose mind was illuminated by Divine Wisdom, — an *Adept*, — who possessed the knowledge of his own Higher Self, all that appears strange and impossible in his character becomes at once clear and comprehensible; but we cannot conceive of him in that light, without entering to a certain extent within the mystic realm of occult science, whose key is the power of spiritual perception, called *Intuition*. Looked at in that light, he stands before us as an ideal Man and as a personification of Divine Wisdom.

The standard of morality and spirituality of a people will always depend on the quality and attitude of the ideals they follow. If their ideals are monstrous and unnatural, they will be vicious and lead unnatural lives; if their ideals are true, they will be guided by considerations of truth. The ideal created by the Spanish monks and which they called their "Christ" was a devil, and their deeds were the actions of devils. The standard of morality and spirituality existing among the various Christian churches of the world, including more than two hundred Christian sects, may be correctly estimated, according to their higher or lower conception of the term "*Christ*." In many cases we find that conception very narrow, and therefore the doctrines of these sects differ in such cases widely from the doctrines of Christ.

"*The Christ*" or "*Messiah*" means the redeeming power of *Universal* spiritual consciousness, love, and intelligence, while the limited "Christ" of the churches is merely a person, whose love manifests itself at best only inside the church. The real Christ means *Universal Life*, while the "Christ" of the sects means separateness and favoritism. True Christianity means spiritual enlightenment, universal benevolence, charity and tolerance; Churchianism means mental darkness, stubborn ignorance, selfishness, intolerance, self-conceit, and hate for all who will not submit to clerical rule. True religion, such as may perhaps be found in the far-distant *golden age*, means that entire renunciation and self-sacrifice, such as we find it described in the *Bhagavad Gita* and in other sacred books of the East, and which is also represented by the ill-understood symbol of the Christian *Cross;* but modern sectarianism, the offspring of the worship of the bloodthirsty Jehovah, is based upon a concentration of all our hopes and aspirations upon the attainment of some selfish personal benefit here or in the hereafter; upon a craving to save that worthless self, even if its salvation were to involve the ruin of the rest of the world.

True religion — the power to know and realize spiritual truths — is attained by those who can rise above the sphere of their illusive self; sectarianism is kept alive and nourished by the love of men for their own animal self and by the fear to lose that beloved thing. As long as this love of self — based upon an entire misconception of the true nature of Man — is not eradicated from the heart of mankind and replaced by knowledge, the Upas-tree of dogmatism will find therein a soil in which to spread its roots and to reap temporal benefits for the church at the expense of the eternal welfare of its deluded adherents.

In *Jehoshua Ben-Pandira* we behold a divinely inspired man. Inspired, — not by any external personal deity, — but by the eternal light of Divine Wisdom, that illumined his mind. We behold in him first a Rabbi, a man of great talents, who sought earnestly after the truth, and who, after having been initiated into the ancient Egyptian mysteries, became a prophet and a seer. Having arrived at a knowledge of the truth, he heroically defended it against the priests of the temple and sacrificed his life in the attempt to bring the life of the true Christ, that existed within himself, to the understanding of the masses. He attempted to dispel the clouds of darkness, created by superstition and fear, so that the light of spiritual knowledge might enter the hearts of mankind. He taught the principle of universal fraternal love, of a love for the sake of love, — not a love on account of expected rewards; but his ideas were too grand, too sublime, to be comprehended by the narrow-minded bigots of his age. He was murdered by those whom he attempted to save, and *He — whose whole life-effort was directed to overthrow the superstitious belief in a limited God, separated from humanity and subject to whims and caprices, — was so little understood by his followers, that, after his death, those who claimed to believe in his teachings, made of himself such a limited god, separated him from humanity, and selected him for an object of their external worship.*

In "*Jesus of Nazareth*" we behold a beautiful allegory, representing the spiritual germ of divine Intelligence in the soul of Man, conceived in the heart by the power of the spirit of Divine Wisdom, continually born in the mystic *Bethlehem* situated in the purest region of the human soul. To speak of Him as an "historical person" is a blasphemy and an absurdity. He never was killed by the Jews, although he is continually crucified by professed Christians. He is alive to-day and will live forever, and resides in the hearts of those who adore him and obey his commands.

Is mankind nowadays better prepared to receive the gospel of the universal saving power of Knowledge and Love than when Jehoshua lived? Are men ready now to do away with the religion of fear and selfishness and substitute for it the gospel of Freedom? Will it now be possible for them to comprehend that their beloved self, to which they cling with the grip of despair, as a drowning man clings to a straw, has no permanent existence at all — but is merely an illusion, a product of a continually changing interaction of correlating forces; which, acting within the physical plane, produce that sensation which causes the illusion of isolated existence? Will the pious be ready to believe, that before they can hope for any immortality of their individual self, they will first have to begin to live by finding that individual *Higher Self*, their *Saviour*, who exists in a life beyond the separation of form? Will they be ready to receive the gospel of eternal and universal life in the spirit, or will they regard a doctrine which denies the immortality of the lower self as being identical with denying the immortality of the *soul?* Have men become intelligent and heroic enough to be free, or must they still be furnished with the crutches of hope and fear to enable them to stand upright? Are men now their own Masters, or are priestcraft and superstition still necessary evils, to keep the ignorant in subjection and terror and to make them obey the law? Is a religion which is based upon the love of men for their animal selves, and whose only excuse for existence is its expediency and usefulness for political and social purposes, really useful in the end? Is such a religion calculated to ennoble mankind, or may perhaps the cause for the growth of selfishness and its resulting evils be found in that spirit of egotism upon which that religion rests? Will it be practicable now to proclaim truths, which have at all times been carefully hidden from the eyes of the ignorant, and if not, should not the truth be told for its own sake and irrespective of any consequences that may result therefrom? Can the knowledge of the truth have any other effect in the end but that of ennobling those who open their eyes to its light, even if the dawn of to-day will cause a temporary disturbance among the dark mists of ignorance which cover the face of the earth?

These important questions seem to be well worthy of our consideration, especially at the present day, when the Christian temples all over the world are seen to totter and shake, because they are built upon sand; when the monsters of anarchism, socialism, nihilism, etc., born of ignorance, rear their heads, and tyranny and monopoly, the offspring of selfishness, are vampirizing humanity; when the whole of Europe appears to be threatened by a devastating war, and America is beginning to suffer the ills produced by causes transplanted from the old world to the new.

In regard to so-called science, the age which seems now to be nearing its end has been one of blind materialism; in regard to so-called religion, it has been one of formalism and credulity in supposed historical facts; but it is said that now has the time arrived when one of the seals of the "closed book" spoken of in the Bible is to be opened; that is to say, that the understanding of mankind as a whole will be opened to a comprehension of eternal truths, which for ages past have been misunderstood.

The following allegories describe the processes which are taking place within the inner or thought-life of all who strive for initiation, and which must have therefore also taken place within the inner life of Jehoshua, if that person was what we may well suppose him to have been,—a man illumined by the spirit of Divine Wisdom.

THE TRUE HISTORY OF CHRIST.

(*AN ALLEGORY.*)

Forever the Light shineth into darkness, but the darkness comprehendeth it not.

LONG, long ago in the past, perhaps millions of ages ago, at a time beyond human calculation, there was a realm of Light, wherein resided the Spirit of Wisdom. His body was like a Sun, and the living rays emanating from him filled the universe with glory. Matter of a fiery and ethereal kind, such as is unknown to man, filled all space, and the light coming from that Spirit penetrated the realm of Matter and endowed it with life and sensation. Gradually this matter began to cool, centres of attractions were formed, and around these centres still more matter condensed, and they grew into revolving globes travelling with lightning velocity through space, being guided by the Spirit of Wisdom. Upon these globes stones, vegetables, animals, and human beings grew.

But in proportion as this matter became dense and solid, it became impenetrable to the light coming from the Spirit of Wisdom, and the men born therein groped in darkness, until they discovered a phosphorescent substance in the caves of the earth which gave forth a light like a diamond after having been exposed to the sun, and they called it "*Ratio.*" By the light of this stone they were able to see their surroundings. Men and animals used this stone, but in the hands of men it shone brighter than when the animals used it.

But the light which they now possessed threw a false glitter upon the objects which it illuminated and caused them to appear distorted and not as they actually were. The Spirit of Wisdom, pitying mankind on account of their ignorance and darkness wherein they lived, resolved to descend to them; but being unable to make himself visible to men, because their eyes had become petrified and blind, he attempted to manifest himself by assuming a more solid shape in their souls.

He entered the Heart of Man and found it to be a stable, filled with animals of all kinds. There was an *ox* called the *Will*, tied to the yoke of passion, and an *ass* called *Reason*, led about by erroneous speculations. There was a *hog* called *Intemperance*, and a *goat* called *Lechery*, and around the door prowled the tiger, the wolf, and the hyena, seeking to gain admittance, while snakes and poisonous reptiles were wriggling and crawling through the cracks of the roof. The stable was full of impurities, the windows were covered with cobwebs, that prevented the light from entering; but in spite of these disgusting surroundings the Spirit of Wisdom remained there and attempted to clean it and transform it into a temple, fit for him to reside therein.

He attempted to make his presence known to the

proprietor of the stable, but for a long time his calls were not listened to; for besides the noise made by the animals in the lower part of the building, there was a great noise made in the upper story, which was occupied by traders of all kinds, by lecturers and preachers, scientists, theologians and moralizers, of whom each one tried to make himself heard above the rest.

By some accident the voice of Wisdom attracted at last the attention of the proprietor, but he could not understand what it said, for the language seemed foreign to him. He therefore sent a commission to examine the claims of that Spirit. *Sophistry* and *Superstition*, the daughters of *Ignorance*, and a fellow named *Logic*, an illegitimate son of a woman called *Experience*, arrived, accompanied by a dog called *Selfishness*. They listened to the Spirit and wrote down what he said. They then asked him for his certificates, to prove who he was, and wanted to dispute with him; and as he did not answer their arguments in a manner comprehensible to them, they shook their heads and did not believe what he said. The animals clamored that the strange visitor should be ejected, for his presence disturbed them in their comfort and ease. Moreover, the angel having begun to assume a material form, needed some nourishment to acquire substance and strength, and he abstracted blood from the animals in the stable and nourished himself with it.

Such a state of affairs appeared intolerable to the proprietor of the house, and he resolved to kill the intruder. He was, however, afraid to attack him openly, because he feared the light that shone from his body. He had in his employ two servants in whom he trusted, although they were *two thieves*, who continually robbed their master of his most valuable treasures whenever any opportunity offered itself; but he knew it not, and believed them to be his faithful assistants. The name of one of these thieves was *Credulity*, and the name of the other was *Scepticism*, and both were the greatest enemies of the *Truth*.

One evening the Spirit went into the garden that surrounded the house. He had succeeded in transforming, by his magic power, some of the animals into men, and they followed him; but the proprietor hearing of his whereabouts, sent his servants to have him arrested. But *Credulity* and *Scepticism* had never seen the Spirit of Wisdom and did not know him; they therefore applied to *Logic*, who by a certain trick of argumentation, which he had learned from a sorceress in the West, whose name was *Curiosity*, managed to come very near to the *Truth*, and kissed him, and (they) then treacherously overpowered the Spirit of Wisdom and caused him to be crucified. But the Spirit, being immortal, could not die; the men who attempted to kill him merely destroyed his form, and thereby rendered themselves incapable of seeing his outward expression, and the Spirit of Wisdom returned to his eternal home, to descend again and again into the hearts of men and to repeat the same process forever and ever, by being born, crucified, and resurrected every day.

"JEHOVAH."

A beautiful god is the most noble product of Man.

MAN-CREATED GODS are most wonderful beings. They possess all the virtues and vices of those who made them, and they in return cause their creators to be vicious or virtuous, foolish or wise. It is known to the student of occult science, that if a man consciously and wilfully performs an act, whether it be good or evil, he calls a living power into existence, which reacts upon him, until the strength with which it has been endowed by him who conjured it up, is exhausted, and while it lives, it may be either a curse or a blessing to its creator. Thus it is even with the creating of gods, and the law that applies to an individual man also applies to a people.

From the time of the Babylonian captivity up to the present day a curse seems to have been attached to the Jewish nation. They have been persecuted in almost every country; they have been hated wherever they went. Justly or unjustly, their cowardice, selfishness, and greed have almost become proverbial; as a nation they have surpassed all others in grasping and hoarding wealth; they are as a whole believed to be tyrannical, unrelenting, and obstinate, while on the other hand they excel other nations in such virtues as grow from a state of separateness and isolation; they closely cling to each other, they assist each other in need; they love their families, and become even heroes in the defence of what they may legally claim as their own.

If we attempt to trace the curse which seems to rest upon them to its origin, we may find it in the fact that they have created that cruel, bloodthirsty, and selfish god, whom they called "Jehovah," and the god whom they had created, reflected upon them his own attributes and became the instrument of their punishment. They materialized a grand idea, forced it into a limited form and endowed it with life, and they thereby chained themselves to that form and became its slaves. In creating a separate god of their own, isolated from the universal God of humanity, they became themselves separated and isolated from the rest of mankind; their god, whose favorites they imagined themselves to be, was the outcome of their own selfishness, and he became the instrument of their torture: the birth of Jehovah became the curse which clung to their heels wherever they went.

For millions of years the eternal *Brahm*, the great and universal Spiritual Sun of Wisdom, had sent his beneficent rays into the world of mind. He knew no distinction of person, but gave the light of wisdom to all who opened their hearts to receive it; the water of Truth descended like rain upon all, and refreshed those who opened their souls to drink it in. Life, Light, and Happiness were accessible to all mankind, without the interference of man-ordained priests; the Universal God asked for no other sacrifice but that which rises up spontaneously from a pure heart, the adoration of absolute Good,—a sacrifice which, kindled by the fire of unselfish Love, rises up like a cloud to the throne of the Eternal and returns again like heavenly dew, showering upon him who offers the sacrifice seven times more of that which he gives.

Thus in ancient times the heaven-ordained priests — that is to say, all human beings who were conscious of the existence of a universal divine ideal — fed the gods with sacrifices of pure and exalted thoughts, and were fed in return by the gods;[1] they sent their spiritual aspirations from the altar of a pure heart into the highest regions of thought and called spiritual forces into action, which reacted upon them, endowing them with knowledge and ennobling their characters. Their "prayers" served to thin the veil of matter by which they were surrounded and to enable them to look beyond the "gates" of their prisons. The higher state of consciousness to which they arose created a new "Jerusalem" in their souls and caused them to realize their own true manhood and their true condition as living, embodied, spiritual powers, kings and lords of creation. They needed no help from external, personal gods; because they were aware of the living presence of the universal Spirit of Wisdom acting within themselves.

[1] Bhagavad Gita, III. 12.

But as with the increase of the population the battle for terrestrial existence became stronger, and men, forced by external circumstances, began to give more attention to their animal necessities than to the requirements of a life in the Eternal, as they became strongly attracted to sensual things, and lost proportionately the power to conceive of that which transcends sensual perception; they became unconscious of their own divine nature, they lost confidence in the divine power within themselves, and clamored for help from external sources. They forgot how to *pray*, and learned how to *beg;* and as no god appeared to give them the things which they desired, they invented gods of their own. They needed gods who promised to save them from slavery, because having become slaves to *Self,* they were now too busy to execute the commands of their master, and to attend to his affairs, to give much attention to their salvation, and to work themselves effectively to recover their freedom. Thus the Unlimited, Eternal, and Infinite disappeared from their view, and in its place they created limited, personal, and changeable gods. The god which the Jews created was called "Jehovah,"—a name whose real meaning was known only to few,—and they endowed him with all the good and evil qualities which characterized their own selves.

Natural and heaven-ordained priests, such as were conscious of the divinity existing in man, and who refused to render homage to man-made gods, were persecuted and slain; divine worship became a matter of trade and was intrusted to man-ordained clergymen, who had no higher ideal than their own semi-animal selves, represented by the gods who were the offspring of their own imagination. The interest of the church became paramount to the acquisition of Wisdom, external ceremonies and material sacrifices took the place of spiritual aspirations and heart-offerings, hopes of future rewards and fears of punishment in the dread hereafter took the place of that nobility of character which seeks to do good for the love of Good, irrespective of any consequences that may accrue to one's self therefrom. External heavens and hells were invented, and the priests truly possessed the keys to them; for by acting upon the imagination of the believers, they could cause them to believe to be either in heaven or in hell. Thus the eternal *Reality*, the *Truth*, was deposed from its throne in the hearts of men, and priest-craft, with its illusions, assumed the sceptre.

When the Jews created their god they lost their own manhood; they lost all confidence in their own power. Thenceforth they trusted in their creature, and the god whose fathers they were, fed them with promises and prophecies, which were never kept nor fulfilled. While the gods of the Romans inspired the latter to perform deeds of valor, this Jewish god promised to accomplish their duties for them. Instead of helping themselves, they now waited for help from their god, and remained slaves, bound by chains of their own construction. But in vain arose to the clouds the odor of burning bullocks and sheep from the altars of the temples; Jehovah had no power to help his worshippers. He was a monster, created by selfishness and needed all he had for himself; he could not give life to the Jews, because his own life depended on the life-energy he received from them; he could not fulfil their expectations, for he had no power but that which was lent to him by his worshippers. (Only when men create gods from whom they expect nothing, will their expectations be fulfilled. When they realize this truth, then will the creating of gods become useless, and men will again become able to find the one true and universal God, who fulfils all his promises by acting in and through the organism of Nature and Man.

As long as men have different desires, they will have different gods; as long as they wander at the base of the mountain with many peaks, each man will believe the peak which is most prominently before him to be the highest of all. Only when they have all arrived at the summit, will they know the highest point; only when they have arrived at the highest conception of the truth, will they begin to know the universal God. They will then see that the gods whom they worshipped before, and who seemed so grand, were only the products of illusions, and that standing on the summit, they—on account of the altitude they occupy—are, as it were, the summit themselves.

By worshipping the gods whom they create, men worship nothing else but themselves. They are creating a mental image, which they endow with their own character; they concentrate upon it their thoughts, their hopes and fears, and as they themselves become old and toothless and wrinkled, they are horrified to see the image in the mirror before them change its features. They discover imperfections about their god, where they had imagined everything to be perfect. They then attempt to "doctor" their god; they apply plasters and salves, they paint him and dress him up, they seek to prolong his life; but the new generations, having a younger ideal, see him putrefy below the varnish and mask: they want a young god, a god that resembles themselves, and they create a new one for themselves.

Thus gods are continually subject to change. As the character of a nation changes, so changes its god. To reform the gods of humanity, humanity must be reformed. Only when all men are of one mind, will they all have the same God.

But that universal ideal which causes all men to be of one mind cannot be found in external creeds, ceremonies, and forms, nor in adjustable opinions and doctrines; for external appearances, opinions, and theories are continually subject to change. Each human being differs from every other in his external appearance and in the way he thinks. There is only one thing which all men share and which constitutes their humanity: it is the consciousness of being human; the knowledge that they are superior to stones, vegetables, and animals, and that they belong to the great family of mankind.

This consciousness does not change as long as men remain human. If they become brutalized they also become unconscious of their dignity as human beings; they then cease to be men and remain human merely in external shape. Likewise, in proportion as men rise up to a realization of what is divine and eternal in man, they become conscious of a higher state of existence; they expand into gods, while they still have the stamp of humanity impressed upon their forms. When all men will have become conscious of this Divine state of existence, then will they all have one common God.

There can be only one *Supreme Cause* of life, consciousness, and wisdom, and its dominion must extend wherever these three factors exist. Men cannot know God as long as they are not divine themselves; but when in the course of evolution mankind will have thrown off the chains which bind them to the attractions of matter, they will again become able to know within themselves the character of the true and universal God, whose wisdom is manifest everywhere in Nature, whose external aspect is visible in all places, but whose power can be realized only by him in whom God has awakened to self-consciousness. Then will men know that God is One and All in All, and that Humanity is spiritually one without separation and division.

Then will a wail arise from the gods that have been created by man, for their end has come. Then will a wail arise from the Pharisees and the scribes who claim to be the keepers of wisdom and messengers of the gods which men have invented; for the gods, the servants of the church, will be useless, and with them their own authority will be at an end. Then will the people cease to sacrifice to the *golden calf*, and the kingdom of the true *Jehovah*, who rejoices within the hearts of men when they kill their animal passions and sacrifice to him their erroneous opinions, will be restored; but those who refuse to open their eyes to the sunlight of truth will remain in darkness and suffer the tortures which they themselves have created by their own morbid imagination.

NAZARETH.

From the conjunction of the Intellect and the Intuition, the Son, whose name is Wisdom, is born.

ONE of the most beautiful countries in Palestine is *Galilee*. It appears like an oasis in the midst of the desolate sunburnt wastes, so frequently seen in the *Holy Land*, and in one of its most charming spots is situated the village of *Nazareth*. Green are the fields and abundant the forests, and in the orchards around the huts composing the village the fig and the lemon grow. To the east is the River Jordan, flowing tranquilly between the gardens and villas situated upon its borders and sparkling in the light of the sun, from the time when that fiery orb rises above towering Mount Tabor until he sinks again below the horizon, behind the cliffs of the Carmel mountains, that loom up in the distant west; while towards the north may be seen a small white strip, the Mediterranean Sea, throwing its foam upon the sandy beach of Phœnicia.

Thus in the mind of man, and in the midst of the wilderness of opinions, a place may be found, deserving the title of "Holy Land," where the river of thought tranquilly flows, illuminated by the Sun of Divine Wisdom, that, ever since the beginning of the world, arose from the East; while in the distant West loom the dark mountains of Scepticism. In that sacred place will the Truth, the true Saviour, be known.

At the beginning of the Christian era the village of Nazareth was a collection of huts, built like all small oriental houses of sun-dried clay, put up apparently without any pretension to design. There were none of those broad avenues and streets, comfortable for walking and driving, which we are accustomed to see where European civilization exists; but there was that charming disorder and variety which gives to ancient towns their peculiar character and endows each spot with a certain amount of individuality of its own. The houses were without windows towards the sides of the street, to keep out intruders, and they received their light from *interior courts*, which in this mild climate served as places for sitting or working during the day and for sleeping apartments at night.

The population of Nazareth, amounting to some four thousand individuals, were for the most part a modest and unassuming people, differing in that respect from the inhabitants of Judea. They were of a mixed kind, consisting of Hebrews, Phœnicians, Arabs, and Greeks, to which were added a number of Roman officers and guards, stationed there for the protection of the interests of the Romans.

As it is usually the case in places where types of various kinds intermingle, the women of Nazareth were very beautiful. They were celebrated on account of their charms all over Palestine; nor could it fail that their beauty attracted the attention of the stately Roman soldiers, and that the latter won the love of the former. Human nature was at those times not fundamentally different from what it is now, and we need therefore not be surprised to hear, that one of the stalwart Roman warriors, whose name was *Pandira*, fell in love with one of the dark-eyed daughters of Nazareth, and that the fruit of their "illegitimate" union was a son, whom they called *Jehoshua*, and who, having inherited from his father the manly pride of the Roman, and from his Jewish mother his almost feminine beauty and modesty, became an appropriate vehicle for the unfolding of that great and powerful spirit of wisdom that inspired him to overthrow the altars of the cruel Jehovah and to teach mankind the gospel of fraternal love.

Let not the pious ear be shocked at the statement that Jehoshua was of illegitimate birth; nor need the "historical" fact that he was born out of wedlock lessen our respect for the great reformer; for it is not often that the truth comes in a manner which is considered legitimate among men. They consider only that knowledge legitimate which has for its parents external observation and logic; but the greatest spiritual truths come by intuition, without external signs. They are the products of interior perception and understanding, and they are rejected as being illegitimate by those who reason from the plane of external effects. They descend silently from heaven, they enter the soul during our dreams; they may be communicated to us in visions and are seen by the spirit, but they are not accepted by the sceptical intellect, which is spiritually blind. The way in which such a knowledge arrives is authorized neither by science nor by the church, for sciences and churches belong to external things, and such truths are therefore rejected by the world.

Only those whose souls are pure and immaculate, whose minds have formed no legalized adulterous alliances with pseudo-scientific and erroneous theological dogmas, only those whose hearts cling to no foreign opinions, but possess within themselves the spirit of knowledge, will be able to receive such illegitimate truths by the power of inspiration. Their souls may become "Mothers of Christ," their minds illuminated by the Holy Spirit of Sanctity, their hearts become living temples of God.

Of Jehoshua's mother little is to be said. Women in oriental countries — then as now — had but little opportunity for receiving an education or for displaying any other accomplishments than their natural talents and physical charms. Ignorant, innocent, and of modest manners, uneducated but kind, sympathetic and beautiful, *Stada*, like many others of her sex, was guided more by the decisions of her heart than by the calculations of her intellect. Her heart yearned for love, and she hoped to find in *Pandira* the realization of her ideal. Her story is a mere repetition of millions of others of the same kind. As in the case of her prototype *Psyche*, her lover departed as soon as she began to find out who he was, and after a period of grief she married a poor citizen, a carpenter, who, on account of her beauty and sweetness of temper, consented to become her husband and a father to her child.

In the family of this *carpenter* and *builder of houses*, Jehoshua passed the days of his childhood, learning to construct *toy-houses* and *cages* for animals. He evidently was a very talented child; for the toy-houses which he constructed were as well adapted for their purposes as the physical form of man is adapted for his soul. While the gospel accounts, whose allegorical language evidently refers to the growth and awakening of the intelligent principle in man, represent Jesus as a supernaturally wise, and therefore unnatural child, the so-called apocryphal gospels speak of him as a wild and mischievous boy, who naturally possessed some powers of black magic, by which he injured his playmates whenever they dared to contradict him or refused to submit to his whims. Considering the latter accounts as having been greatly exaggerated, we may well suppose that, having inherited from his father the temperament of a soldier, he found but little taste in following the profession of his foster-father, and preferred roaming about the neighborhood of the village and a stroll to the mountains, to handling the saw at the carpenter's bench. The illegitimate and therefore unwelcome son of the carpenter's wife was not overestimated or unduly fondled at home, and many a little storm arose in that peaceful house in the village of Nazareth on account of the roaming habits of that boy who loved to stroll away from the village at night, to climb among the rocky recesses of the Carmel mountains, or to sit on moonlight nights upon a cliff, looking out upon the wide expanse of the Mediterranean Sea, dreaming of countries which he had never seen, and wondering what shores were upon the other side of the water.

A schoolhouse may be a good place to educate the Intellect and to bring it to an understanding of external phenomena; but for the expansion of the spiritual *Intelligence* and the ennobling of character, Nature herself is the best teacher. Great is the superiority of the educated and learned mind over the uneducated; but still greater is the light of those who have been taught by Nature herself, and acquired wisdom independently of the instruction of mortals. Those who spend their lives in schools often acquire a great deal of information in regard to external things, which may be very useful as far as it goes, while at the same time they may lose the capacity to perceive internal and fundamental truths, which are far more important than all they may possibly learn in regard to phenomenal existence. Why is it that often shepherds, hunters, and fishermen, and those who spend their lives in the solitudes of the mountains, the forest, or the ocean are capable of conceiving of very exalted ideas, far beyond the intellectual grasp of the dogmatist? Is it perhaps that the spirit of man, beholding by means of the senses the wide expanse of Nature, is attracted towards the Infinite and Eternal, his legitimate home, and thus loosens the chains that bind him to his terrestrial prison, and thins the veil which prevents men from looking into the realm of the Unknown? Little does our modern civilization know about that grand school in which the universal spirit of Divine Wisdom is teacher, where the heart expands and the mind conceives ideas too grand to be expressed in the language of mortals; but often, when the physical body is resting in sleep and the intellectual powers of man cease to watch, the spirit, loving his freedom, may steal away from his labor of building his toy-prison house, and roam about in the regions of his eternal home, until he is called back by the awakening senses, to attend to his terrestrial labors.

While rambling through the fields and forests of Galilee the mind of Jehoshua expanded and began to stretch its feelers towards the realm of the Eternal. Often while entering into meditation, half-forgotten memories of previous lives passed upon this planet, flitted before his soul, and indistinct images of the future presented themselves to his spiritual vision. What is *"memory"* but a power to recollect and spiritually perceive the images of the past impressed upon the *Astral Light?* and may not our spirit as it expands and increases in power, not only remember its own previous existences upon this globe, but read in the *memory of Nature* the whole history of the world? A yearning to know the

Unknown filled his soul, and his mind, not being crammed with adopted opinions, drank wisdom from the universal fountain of truth.

As he grew up, the political and religious questions of those times began to attract his attention. Being a Hebrew with Roman blood in his veins, he shared neither the intolerance and hate of the Jews against their oppressors, nor the contempt with which the latter regarded the former, and this fortunate circumstance helped to a great extent to develop in his soul the germs of religious and political toleration, and to cause them to grow and expand into that love for all humanity without distinction of race and religious opinion, whose representative he became later on.

Why do men quarrel about their opinions in regard to religion? Has not every one a right to believe what he pleases, as long as he has no knowledge? When real knowledge, such as results from a direct perception and understanding, arrives, then there can be no more quarrelling about theories. If a blind man were to deny to one who sees that the latter is able to see, the seer would hardly care to argue with the blind, nor would he be likely to convince him; for real knowledge cannot be taught, it must be gained by experience. What we learn without experiencing it, is merely a matter of opinion. He who quarrels with another in regard to opinions is after all merely quarrelling with his own doubts.

Quietly and monotonously passed the days at Nazareth;

there was but *little trade* carried on in that place. Agricultural occupations and the vintage were the things that took up the attention of the inhabitants; but the great event of the year was, when at the time of the festival of the "*Tabernacles*" and "Passover" the country population went to Jerusalem, to enjoy the sights of the capital and to attend to the customary religious observances. On such an occasion the streets of the capital resembled a fair; the houses were filled with strangers, and on the outside of the city walls camps were put up, where, sheltered by tents and straw-covered huts, the pilgrims cooked their meals and discussed the events of the day.

On such occasions the great temple was crowded from morning till night. Traders of all kinds filled the courts, and even into the sanctuary penetrated the noise of the merchant praising his goods and disputing about the price with the buyer; while in the interior of the temple equally greedy Pharisees sold theological creeds and promises of heavenly rewards to the believers. Some of the halls were devoted to the distribution of justice, and in other halls learned discussions were held. There the letter of the Law was explained with lengthy arguments and elaborate sophistry, while the spirit of the ancient doctrines was denied and driven away. The secret meaning of these doctrines was known to few, and those who knew it were looked upon as being heretics and persecuted by the orthodox adherents of the church.

Thus the temple at Jerusalem resembled the mind of

man, where a continual warfare is going on between the interests of the lower animal and reasoning self, and the dictates of divine wisdom are not listened to. In the mind of man, as in the temple of Jerusalem, there exists a continual struggle between conflicting opinions, between selfish desires of different kinds, between doubt and superstition, hope and fear, and the Scribes and Pharisees appealing to the selfish propensities in the constitution of man, often assert their borrowed authority and overpower the truth by means of sophistry and an erroneous application of logic.

Jehoshua was frequently present during those learned disputations. His natural common sense revolted at the sophistry of the Pharisees, by which they perverted the truth, and taking part in the discussions he disconcerted them by his questions and confounded their logic. The intrepidity and intelligence he manifested on such occasions attracted the attention of *Rabbi Perachia*, a former president of the *Sanhedrin*, who was more intelligent and liberal than his colleagues. He invited Jehoshua to his house and became his instructor. A strong friendship grew up between the old man and the boy, and as the former was about to visit Egypt for the purpose of prosecuting certain researches in the sciences called *occult*, he invited Jehoshua to accompany him on that voyage, and the latter gladly accepted the offer.

EGYPT.

Man, after having vainly sought for the light of the Truth in externals, and found nothing but darkness, at last discovers that the land of the sunrise exists within his own soul.

Hail thee, O Egypt, thou sanctuary of ancient mysteries, thou land of magic and wonders! When the truth was driven away from its birthplace in the East by the king of all evils, the love of Self, it found a refuge with thee. Thy indestructible books hold the records of ancient wisdom, and sectarian bigotry has in vain sought to destroy them. With thee they will rest safely, until selfishness dies and men wake up to a consciousness of their freedom. Then will the truth return to them, and they may re-enter the Holy Land of Knowledge.

In vain the powers of darkness have attempted to silence the voice of the truth that speaks through thy stony lips. Sectarian Vandals have broken thy tablets and plastered up thy hieroglyphics; but thy stones cry out and proclaim the gospel of wisdom. Men have carried away thy monuments, and they have become messengers of light from the East to the West. No more is thy ancient wisdom taught in subterranean caves to the initiated; thy secrets have been profaned by the profane; thy sacred pearls have been thrown before the swine of superstition and to the dogs of blind scepticism; but the swine and the dogs turned away from the pearls and devoured only the dirt with which the treasures were covered. Men have robbed thy temples of precious gold, but the gold which they found turned to ashes in the hands of the selfish, because they did not know its true value. They went to the fountain of truth, to drink of its waters; but their cups were not purified. They communicated to the water their own impurities, and it became a poison to them, causing villanous leprosy, which they communicated to others. They penetrated to the ark that contained the mystery, but they had no key to unlock it; so they carried away the ark and exhibited it in the West, but the mystery remained in Egypt.

To thee, O Egypt, the true Redeemer was known; not as a man made deity, or as a figure in history; but as the Spirit of Truth, constituting all that is immortal in man. Thy Knowledge was too grand to be grasped by the pigmies that invaded thy soil, desecrated thy temples, profaned thy sanctuaries, travestied the truths which were taught and made of a sacred myth, that teaches an eternal truth an historical falsehood.

Who can enter an Egyptian temple or even look at one of these ancient monuments, without feeling a sensation of awe and solemnity, which few Christian cathedrals, with their puppets, manikins, and tinsel, will ever produce? How far more grand and sublime than our modern misconceptions must have been a religion that expressed itself in such gigantic forms! Who but an animal can behold these pyramids, the symbols of immensity, whose bases rest upon the earth, and whose points reach up to heaven, without feeling the oppression of Matter and the desire of the Spirit for freedom? Who can behold these monuments of a forgotten past, without sensing the presence of that consciousness which fills all space, the Spirit of God still floating over the waters, without limits, indivisible, all in all, present everywhere and pervading every atom?

Is there any soul in so-called inanimate things, and if not, what causes these stones to speak to our inner consciousness with a voice much louder than that of the occupant of a pulpit? Is it perhaps that the Truth itself is speaking to us through these stones, while the pulpit orator merely repeats what he has learned, and is therefore merely an echo of the opinions of fallible men?

Have stars souls, or are they merely dead aggregations of matter? and if they are without souls, what is the force that keeps their atoms together and guides their revolutions in space? Why is Supreme Wisdom — a wisdom beyond the conception of Man — everywhere manifest in Nature, if in Nature no consciousness exists? If Nature is an unconscious thing, how can Wisdom exist without Consciousness and Intelligence? Is Nature a product of Life, or Life a product of Nature? and must there not be a Consciousness of some kind, wherever is Life? Is it not reasonable to suppose that what we call "Motion" is a manifestation of Life, and that what we call "Matter" is endowed by the universal Spirit with a certain amount of Life, and that the life of different forms differs in its manifestation merely according to the organization of the Matter composing the forms? If this is true, then there is no inorganic matter of any kind to be found in the forms of nature, but stones and rocks must have organizations of their own, and each planet its own peculiar life, differing from the life of other stars in the treasury vault of heaven.

If this view is seen to be correct, then will the apparently dead universe, with its unconscious motion and its causeless mechanical laws, be transformed into a thing of life, pervaded with invisible but living and conscious powers, guided by one eternal unchangeable Law originating in divine Wisdom. Then will those dead globes of matter, floating in space and obeying mechanical laws for some unexplainable reason, be changed into a living family of children of the universal God, who are all doing the will of their Father, because it is their Father's will that endows them with life.

But if the suns and stars and all the so-called inanimate things have life, then they must have some kind of consciousness and sensation, even if they are not self-conscious and have no knowledge of individual separate life. They may be subject to loves and hates, to desires and passions, to attractions and repulsions. Then it would seem that the ancient Astrologers were right after all in attributing certain virtues and vices to the different planets and stars and in believing in a certain kind of interchange between their radiations. There is no reason why stars should not be in possession of Intelligence, even if they are not conscious that they are existing as separate beings. Is it not possible that even a high degree of Consciousness and Intelligence may exist in an organism that is not aware of the fact of being an entity different from other entities in the Universe?

Let us here ask the question, whether a high state of consciousness and intelligence is not possible even in Man without any consciousness of *Self*. Are not men most happy when they forget their own selves? Do they not, when they become interested in reading a book or in witnessing a theatrical performance, listening to music, etc., forget for the time being that they are entities existing separately from others? Do men not even drink the intoxicating cup for the purpose of forgetting Self, and are they not miserable in proportion as they think of themselves? Men do not cease to live or to think, to be intelligent, to know, to love, and to will, when they forget their own Self; but they then cease to have selfish thoughts, a self-will, and a selfish imagination. If we could be free forever from that sensation of Self, we would not cease to be conscious and intelligent and happy; but we would cease to be limited by that self, and we would all do the will of the universal God and partake of his thoughts.

Perhaps a glance at the ancient books of Wisdom may throw some light upon this matter.

If we open the Bible, the first verse of the first chapter of *Genesis* teaches us a great truth, taught by the Egyptian Hierophants: "*Bereschit bara Elohim, ath ashamain on ath aoris.*" This is to say: "The First Cause produced the powers which constitute heaven and earth."[1] If the First Cause produced all beings, even those that have life, it must be itself the source of all Life. If it produced the powers which constitute Wisdom, it must be Wisdom itself. If the *Great First Cause* is Spirit, — and what else can we call it? — then by producing all things it endowed them with its own spirit, and all things must have a spiritual basis, which enables them to exist. All things must have "souls," and it is their souls which cause their material constituents to act upon each other, and produce the divine harmony which we observe throughout Nature.

Where do the material constituents of a being end? Are they all enclosed within the shell of its visible form, or may there not be invisible radiations of sensitive "matter," not having entered the solid form, but nevertheless belonging to its organization? Does not the *Corona* of the sun belong to its substance as much as the fiery globe constituting his inner body? Does not the power which a magnet exercises at a distance belong to the magnet? May we not look upon a star as being

---

[1] The term "heaven" refers to all states of consciousness; "earth," to all forms of matter.

an organized body, whose periphery extends as far as its influence reaches, while its visible globe is merely the visible kernel of the great invisible mass, and may not the same reasoning be applied to all living beings, even to Man? If this is true, then we are all — like the stars — living within the spheres of each other, and all beings are substantially *one*, separated from each other merely by the illusion of form.

It is very difficult for man, whose perceptions are subject to the limitation imposed by form, to conceive of the invisible and formless; but he will never be able to obtain the key to the understanding of the divine mysteries of nature, until he realizes the *Unity* of the *All*, and knows that the so-called invisible and unknowable realm is the real and substantial world, while the great phantasmagoria of corporeal forms is merely an illusion, produced by aggregations of matter and constructed by the *souls of things*, the *carpenters* in the workshop of Nature; the step-fathers of the newly-begotten son of Divine Wisdom.

It is known that the ancient Egyptians were well versed in Astronomy, and recent discoveries made in regard to the construction of the Great Pyramid go to show that they knew in many respects more about this science than the moderns suspect; but to them the suns and planets were representing invisible realities. To them the visible corporeal stars were merely external manifestations of invisible internal powers. Where the present civilization beholds nothing else but dead material bodies, obeying the mechanical law of *gravitation*, whose cause it cannot explain, the ancient Egyptians beheld a universe filled with life, following the universal law of order and harmony, whose cause is the Will of the eternal Creator, who produced these forms within the substance of his own Mind.

The visible terrestrial sun was to them a representation of the invisible spiritual *Central Sun* of Divine Wisdom, named the Sun-God *Osiris* (Christ), unknowable to *external* sensation, but manifesting itself as *Horus* (Jesus) in the hearts of mankind; becoming "regenerated" within the souls of the pure by the power of our eternal Mother, *Isis*, the ever immaculate *virgin*, the goddess of Nature. "God" to them was not a limited being, but the Eternal Cause of all manifestations of power within the realm of Matter and in the kingdom of Spirit, containing within himself everything that exists, and yet in consciousness being superior to all beings. While all things are living and changing in him, he remains always the same; tranquil in his eternal glory and undisturbed by any external influence. He does not descend to us, but the gifts which we receive from Him differ according to the positions we occupy in regard to Him.

Let those who desire to know whether these doctrines are true look within their own minds, for Man is an image of his creator. There they will find a continually changing region of thoughts. Subjective forms of all kinds throng that interior realm, ever changing, and without rest. But if they penetrate deeper, even within the realm of the spirit within, they will find a tranquil place and a principle whose state of consciousness is not affected by the changes going on in the mind, and yet these changes are produced by that principle, sending its rays into the world of ideas existing within the mind. (The divine spirit in Man does not descend to the sphere of man's intellectual understanding; but Man may rise up to it in his thoughts.) There are periodical changes taking place in the mind of man, similar to the astronomical changes in the universe. There are ebbs and tides of thought, as there are ebbs and tides of the ocean. There are times when Man involuntarily approaches nearer to God, and times when he recedes. The Egyptians knew that all the mental processes going on in the mind of Man are images on a small scale of the processes taking place on a grand scale in the Universal Mind, and that external phenomena are the shadows of internal realities. Being aware of the unity of the All and knowing the nature of the spiritual forces in the Macrocosm of Nature and their correspondences in the Microcosm of Man, they studied the position of the stars, to know the time when Humanity would again approach nearer to the divine Sun of Wisdom. They were able to tell the changes occurring in the spiritual condition of mankind by studying the position of the visible sun to the *Zodiac*.

But we are entering here upon forbidden ground. Even if we were able to expose the sacred mysteries of the ancient Egyptians to the scoffer and sceptic, it would be a sacrilege to attempt it. Moreover, these mysteries cannot be explained; they are beyond the intellectual conception of mortals. They can only be perceived intuitively by the spiritual intelligence of Man after he has become self-conscious of the divinity of his God.

These sacred mysteries were in the possession of the *Holy Brotherhood*, and they were taught only to those select few who were fit to be instructed in them; or, to express it more correctly, they were not taught at all, but the candidate was instructed how to act, so that his own spiritual powers of perception might be developed within him, and he become able to see and know such things himself. To be admitted within the sacred precincts of the *Crata Repoa*, it was necessary, not only to lead a blameless life, but to be in possession of extraordinary talents and strength of character, and to devote one's life entirely to the practical application of the truths that were taught in this order.

There were several degrees in that fraternity, and no one was admitted as a member of a higher degree until he had completely mastered all that was to be acquired in the lower degrees, and which sometimes required many years to accomplish. An initiation in that order or a passing to a higher degree, was a terribly serious matter, having nothing whatever in common with the sham-initiations, mummeries, idle ceremonies, and ill-understood mysteries of modern secret societies. It was exceedingly difficult to be admitted as a candidate, and still more difficult to pass through the prescribed trials, which were rather of an internal than of an external character. Many of those who did not succeed in standing the tests imposed upon them became insane; others paid with their life the penalty for their daring, or had to remain prisoners in subterranean caves until death came to release them.

Jehoshua applied for admission to one of the members, but was refused; he applied a second time to another member, but was refused again; but after he had applied for the third time, to his great joy he was admitted as a candidate for probation, and he entered the temple at the day appointed for his preliminary instruction.

THE MYSTERIOUS BROTHERHOOD.

There is nothing more difficult to find than one's own self.

AFTER Jehoshua had entered the Egyptian temple, he was led into the presence of the assembled priests. They questioned him in regard to his object in desiring to enter their order, and admonished him to desist; warning him of the dangers that he was to incur, if he insisted in pursuing this way to obtain knowledge of the secret sciences and to come in possession of the powers which such a knowledge conveyed. They told him that if he were once admitted, there would be no possibility to retreat, as he would have to succeed or to lose his freedom and perhaps even his life; for powers of evil which would be aroused would conquer him, unless he were strong enough to conquer them.

Jehoshua Ben-Pandira was not to be intimidated; he desired to obtain knowledge and considered wisdom to be more valuable than life. He insisted upon being admitted. He received the blessings of the Brothers, and as each of these venerable men laid his hands upon his head, he felt an electric thrill pass through his frame, that seemed to invigorate him and to give him a power sufficient to overcome all dangers. After this he was given over to a guide called *Thesmophores*, who blindfolded him and led him away.

He went with his guide through several long corridors, from whose walls the echoes of their steps resounded, and they descended a flight of stairs until at last they arrived at the place of their destination. When the hood was removed, Jehoshua found himself in a cave hewn in the solid rock. It was a high arched vault with massive pillars, cut in a manner to represent figures of men and fabulous animals. The only light which entered into the vault came through a round opening far up in the roof, where a small part of the clear blue sky could be seen. Upon the walls of that prison were written proverbs and mottoes, consisting of extracts from the books of the Egyptian and Indian sages who may have lived in the far-distant past, perhaps even in prehistoric times, when that which we now call Europe formed the bottom of the sea, and another continent was at the height of its civilization at a place where now the ocean rolls its waves.

The room was furnished in the most primitive fashion, containing merely the most necessary requisites. The Thesmophores told the candidate—for such he had now become—that he would have to remain here in solitude for an indefinite period of time. He advised him to occupy himself with thinking of the nature of man and his destiny and to meditate about his own self. He gave him some writing materials and requested him to write down the thoughts that would enter his mind and seem important to him, and after taking leave of the prisoner and wishing him good success, the guide went away.

Thus when the free spirit seeking for knowledge sends its feelers into the tomb of living clay, blindly following the law of reincarnation, he finds himself alone without a guide, left to his own thoughts, and with only a faint light above coming from his former home, while on the walls of the prison house called the Mind, he may find dim recollections of the teachings of wisdom acquired in previous lives.

Jehoshua was now alone. There is nothing more terrible than isolation and solitude to those who know of no other life but that of external sensation and who cannot create their own thoughts; especially if there is no change in their surroundings, to attract their attention and to stimulate them to think. Thinking is an art, and few can think what they wish or hold on to a thought. Men only think what they must; they feed on the ideas that enter their minds without asking. Welcome and unwelcome thoughts enter; they neither come at our bidding nor go away when they are not wanted: they are like disorderly guests that do not obey the rules which the landlord prescribes.

The monotony in which Jehoshua lived remained unchanged. There was no sound of any kind to be heard; he was surrounded by silence; and if it had not been for the small opening in the vault far above his head, he would not have known the changes of day and night. He studied the writings upon the walls, and impressed them upon his memory, analyzing their meaning; and the more he thought about them, the more his mind seemed to expand and new ideas enter. He could not tell from whence they came, but he wrote them down upon the tablets with which he had been provided; and often when in the morning he awoke from his slumber, these tablets had disappeared from his prison, and he knew not what had become of them. He saw no one enter the room, and yet somebody must have taken them away. Likewise the food with which he was provided was supplied by invisible means. It was of the most simple kind, consisting of bread, milk, fruit, and water. It was daily brought to him in some inexplicable manner; how or by what means he could not tell, for it was put into his prison during his sleep. However, he soon ceased to be astonished at such strange occurrences and he began seriously the study of self. As he became accustomed to look within his own soul, a new world seemed to open before him; his imagination grew stronger, and the pictures presented before his inner eye became as objective and real to him as the objects of the external world, only more beautiful, more ethereal, and yet far more substantial than the latter. Visions of things which he had formerly seen, but which had apparently been lost to his memory, appeared again, vivid and real with all their living details; desires entering his heart immediately took objective forms in his mind, representing in seemingly living forms the objects of which he thought, and thus he saw many beautiful things in his visions, but also many horrible sights, for no man is without evil, and evil thoughts that came to him were likewise represented in seemingly real but horrible forms.

What is this plastic power of the imagination, and what do men mean by calling subjective images "*merely works of imagination*"? Can we imagine anything that does not exist? (Are the creations of our thoughts less real to us than the things which the imagination of others created for us?) Is not the universe a product of the imagination of God, and are we not gods in our own inner world, able to create forms from the substance called the *Astral Light?*

Gradually Jehoshua began to love this inner life, where he found a world as large as the outer world, with a space as infinite as that of the latter, with mountains and plains, with oceans and rivers, and peopled with beings of various kinds that looked up to him as their god, their creator, drawing life from his Will, and nourishment from his Thought, in the same sense as Man receives his will-power and ideas from the God in the universe, appearing to him in his dreams while asleep, and in visions while awake. Thus Jehoshua lived in the world of the *Elemental Powers* of Nature, and began to know the constituent parts of that organism called the human soul.

Weeks, perhaps months, thus passed away. Who knows how long he remained in that tomb? He kept no record of the days and nights since he had entered there, and what is time and space, after all, but merely mental conceptions by which we attempt to measure the Infinite? But one day steps were heard to approach; the door which had been closed so long opened, and the Thesmophores entered, congratulating him on his success and inviting him to come to the *Portal of Man*, to enter as a *Neophyte* into the first degree of the holy Brotherhood.

They entered a large park, through which they passed, until they arrived at an entrance called the *Door of the Profane*. There they found a great many people assembled who had been attracted by curiosity to see the new candidate for initiation, for such a rare event was not kept secret, as it was desired that the people should know that there were still men to be found ready to dare all dangers in search of the truth. They thronged the place in front of the door through which Jehoshua passed with his guide, on his way to the Temple of Wisdom; they shouted and made much noise, obstructing the way; but the Thesmophores drove them back, and they passed safely through the crowd.

Having entered the vestibule of the temple, the candidate was taken to a *Crypt*, where he took a bath, and received new garments, and underwent the prescribed preparation to be introduced to the assembly of the Brothers.

The *Portal of Man* was guarded by the *Pastophores*, who, as they arrived, inquired about their purpose and asked Jehoshua various questions. Having received satisfactory replies, the door opened, and he entered a large hall, wherein in a semicircle were seated the Brothers, and in their midst the *Hierophant*. Before this assembly Jehoshua again passed an examination, answering numerous questions in regard to his subjective experiences during his isolation.[1]

He was then led around the *Bisantha*, and there the strength of his nerves and his physical courage, by certain methods which cannot be made intelligible to the modern reader, because they involved an employment of certain forces of nature, the secret of which was in the possession of the *Atlanteans* and *Egyptians*, but whose very existence is as yet unknown to western civilization. It may be sufficient to say, that if claps of thunder resounded and bolts of lightning seemed to strike the candidate,[2] they were not produced in the manner employed in theatrical performances upon the stage, but they were the effects of natural forces, set into action by the occult powers possessed by the Egyptian Adepts. The most horrible spectres appeared, but Jehoshua was not afraid.

Having successfully passed through this trial, he was again taken before the assembly, and the *Menies* read to him the laws of the *Crata Repoa*, which, after due examination, he solemnly promised to obey.[3] By a certain

---

[1] *Plutarch* in Læon. "Apoph. verb. Lysand."
[2] *Eusebius'* Cæsar, Preparat. Evangel.
[3] *Alexander ab Alexandro*, Lib. V. Cap. 10.

process known to the *Hierophant*, his spiritual vision was then opened; that is to say, he was endowed for a short time with the powers to see certain spiritual verities represented in allegorical forms. He found himself standing between *two square columns*, called *Betiles*, and there was a *ladder with seven steps*[1] and *eight closed doors*.[2] As he beheld that vision, its meaning was at once clear to him, for spiritual visions differ from mere dreams especially in so far that he who beholds a symbolical vision becomes at the same time aware of its meaning, else it would be useless to show such a vision to him. In that short moment, during which his inner sight was opened, Jehoshua learned to know the fundamental principles of the Cosmos, a science which would require many months of instruction to be described in words and to be brought to the understanding of the not self-luminous intellect.

The Hierophant then spoke as follows: "I am speaking only to you who have the right and the power to hear me. Firmly close all the doors[3] and exclude all the profanes, the sophists and scoffers[4]; but you, children of the celestial labor,[5] hear my words: Beware of passions and evil desires; beware of erroneous opinions and intellectual prejudices. Keep your mind continually directed toward the divine source of all existence, strive after a continual realization of the presence of

---

[1] *Eusebius'* Demonstr. Evang. Lib. I.
[2] *Origines* cent. Cels. p. 341.
[3] The external senses.
[4] Prejudices.
[5] Spiritual perception.

the Supreme; and if you desire to walk upon the Path of Light to eternal Happiness, do not forget for even one moment, that you are living in the consciousness of Him whose power has created the world. He is all things, and all things are in Him. He is self-existent, pure knowledge, pure wisdom; and although He is seen by no man, there is nothing within the Universe that can hide itself from His sight." [1]

Jehoshua had now become a member of the Egyptian Brotherhood. He was taught the laws of Nature, and made to see that there is nothing *dead* in Nature, but that all forms are manifestations of the one universal power of Life. He was taught the causes of the physical phenomena occurring in the world of phenomena, the nature of Light and Sound, of Heat and Electricity, etc. He was also instructed in Astronomy and Medicine and in the science of Hieroglyphics.[2]

The spiritual nature of Man was explained to him and the laws of Reincarnation. How the human monad again and again descends to build up a mortal physical form and to evolve a new personality at each of its visits upon this globe; that the human forms, which we know as men, women, and children, are not the real Man, but merely ever-changing aggregations of matter, endowed with an ever-changing consciousness, unsubstantial although living illusions, doomed to perish when the Spirit retires to its home, to rest from its labor;

---

[1] *Eusebius'* Preparat. Evangel. I. i. 3.
[2] *Jamblichus*, In Vita Pythagor.

while the substantial, indivisible, and incorruptible Spirit is the *real* Man, although invisible to the perception of mortals.

He was taught the signification of the sacred syllable AUM[1] and of certain symbolical signs,[2] including the double-interlaced *Triangle*, the *Snake*, and the *Tau*, and his office was to guard the *Portal of Man*, so that nothing impure would enter; for no one was ever admitted into the sanctuary of the inner temple, unless he first proved himself a faithful guardian of that door by which evil thoughts and desires attempt to enter the mind.

A year or more may have thus passed away, when the new Pastophores obtained permission to enter the second degree, called *Necoris*. As a preparation for this degree he had to undergo a severe fasting, after which he was introduced into a grotto, called *Endymion*.

This grotto was furnished in a luxuriant manner. It was without windows, but lamps that were suspended from the ceiling, and fed with perfumed oil, shed a soft light through the room. The richest food and the most delicious wines were set before the candidate, and he was invited to partake; for now — so they told him — he had won the victory, and he might now indulge in sensual pleasures without any risk of sin. The most beautiful maidens waited upon him, and their bewitching smiles told him that he had only to mention a wish, to

---

[1] *Plutarch*, De Iride et Osiride.
[2] *Jamblichus*, In Vita Pythagor.

see it fulfilled. It was evident that he was an object of admiration to them, and that they were willing to be his slaves.

But Jehoshua resisted their tempting wiles. His aspirations were for something far higher than the gratification of sensual appetites; the beauty of corporeal form, however pleasing it may be to the eye, could not enslave him who had learned to know the beauty of the Spirit, and as the evening approached, the fair tempters, with looks full of disappointment and unfulfilled desire, disappeared one after another, and Jehoshua, after securely locking the door, threw himself upon a couch.

While he was meditating there, a slight noise attracted his attention, and he saw one of the most beautiful females that mortal eye ever beheld, entering through a secret door, whose existence had escaped his observation. She was of most noble appearance and stately form, clad in loose, flowing garments, and with a sparkling diadem upon her head. Thus may have looked the chaste goddess Diana, when she watched the sleeping Endymion. An expression full of pity and love rested upon her face, as she approached the couch where Jehoshua rested.

"Fear nothing," she said; "I do not come to tempt, but to save thee. I am the daughter of the guardian of this temple, and I have learned the danger which is threatening thee. Dost thou not know that these villanous priests have resolved to kill thee? for thou hast forfeited thy life by learning some of their mysteries. Thou, a foreigner, hast learned secrets which no one but the Egyptians are permitted to know. This evening they have resolved to kill thee, and the murder is to be executed even to-night. I have come to save thee; I have made sure thy escape: rise and follow me, for I admire thy valor and I do not wish thee to perish."

"Beautiful one," answered Jehoshua, "I will not dispute thy words; but if the priests have resolved to kill me, let them do so; for I have promised to obey the laws of this brotherhood, and I have no right to escape."

"Is there not," answered the temptress, "a higher law than the laws made by these priests? Is there not the law of nature, superior to all other laws? Does not the law of thy nature permit and command thee to save thy life?"

"Spare thy words," answered Jehoshua. "I know my duty. I shall remain and await whatever my fate may be."

"Then," said the lady, "I must tell thee what my modesty forbids me to say. It is not the life of a fugitive that I came to offer to thee, but a life of unbounded love, a life of happiness and of luxury. Yes," she continued after a pause, drawing still nearer to him and putting her soft white hand upon his shoulder, "I love thee. Look into my eyes and see whether or not what I am telling is true. Wilt thou bury thy manhood in these living tombs, to seek after things which exist merely in thy imagination? Come with me, and I will give thee a substantial happiness far superior to any that thou mayest find within these gloomy walls. Can there be any greater happiness for a man than the love of a beautiful woman? I am rich, I am free, I am beautiful; I love thee with all the passionate love of which woman is capable. Come with me, and thou shalt never repent it."

"Fair one," answered Jehoshua, "all the earthly elements of my material nature are striving to fly to thy embrace; but they are held by the superior will of the spirit. I do not seek for happiness within these walls, nor could I find contentment in the things which thou offerest to me. I seek for happiness in that which is not subject to change; that which thou canst give is subject to decay. I reject thy offer."

"Dare to reject it!" answered the woman. "Dost thou know what a woman whose love is spurned can do? I shall not leave thee, for my soul clings to thee; to be separated from thee would be death!" As she spoke these words, she drew a dagger from her belt and pointed it to her breast. "Spurn my love," she said, "and this weapon will enter my heart! I will not live without thee; but if I die, my death will also cost thee thy life; for if my dead body is found in this grotto to-morrow, thou wilt be accused of being my murderer, and be executed for it." Seeing that her threats had no effect upon the Neophyte, she threw the dagger upon the floor, and, sinking down at his feet, implored him for his love. She tore away her veil, and her luxuriant hair dropped over her shoulders; tears streamed from her eyes, and her appeals ended in sobs.

"Depart!" sternly answered Jehoshua, and the fair one arose and retreated; but as she disappeared from sight, another door opened, and a stream of light entered the room. The Hierophant and some of the Brothers appeared at the entrance, and, congratulating him on the victory which he had gained, they led him to a large hall, where, after submitting to the ceremony of baptism, he was pronounced to be worthy to be admitted to a higher degree.

Thus should he, who is the guardian of the door, beware that no *secret entrance* is left open, by which a favorite passion may enter; and if the temptress should enter unaware, during his slumber, he should call to his aid the superior power of his awakened Will, and repel her. Then will the door of his soul open, Reason will enter and guide him by the light of Divine Wisdom nearer to permanent Peace.

THE MYSTERIOUS BROTHERHOOD.

(*Continued.*)

To learn the mysteries of the Spirit, we must descend into the subterranean caves where the treasures are hidden.

AFTER a few days of rest and contemplation, Jehoshua was told that the time had arrived when his courage and daring would have to undergo a severe trial. His eyes were again blindfolded, and he was taken to a subterranean cave, into which he had to descend by means of a ladder. Having arrived at the bottom, he removed the bandage from his eyes, according to the directions he had previously received; but he could see no light. The cavern was dark, and at first he could not discern any objects; but he heard hissing sounds close by his side. He made a few steps in advance, and stepped upon a living thing that was gliding over the floor, and which immediately wriggled itself around his leg. Then the fact immediately came to his consciousness that he was in a den of serpents, and that to faint would mean to be lost. Gradually his eyes became accustomed to the deep darkness, and he discerned the eyes and forms of the reptiles that lurked in all the corners. The cavern seemed to be filled with snakes of all kinds. Twisted together in disgusting knots, some were lying on the floor, and others wormed themselves over the rocks. He seated himself upon a stone, and soon the snakes began to approach, as if to resent his presence. They crawled over his legs, twisted themselves around his arms and all over his body.

At first Jehoshua was horrified; but his horror was only of a moment's duration, for he immediately called to his aid his higher consciousness and remembered that his terrestrial form, subject to the disgusting embraces of the crawling reptiles, and made of the same stuff as they, was not his real Self, but merely a form to which he — the divine Man — was for the time being attached. This thought enabled him to look upon everything that might happen to his body as if he were an independent spectator. In this way he appealed for aid to his own God, and as he did so, a superior strength, a power unknown before, seemed to pervade his whole body, and now it seemed as if this power had invested him with some property that made him repulsive to the serpents; for soon the reptiles that were in contact with his body left him and retired into their holes.

Thus if man descends to the innermost depths of his soul, he may find it infested with poisonous serpents and venomous reptiles, the symbols of the brood of passions and evil desires; but if he calls to his aid the divine spirit of Wisdom, the persecutions will cease and peace will return.

After having passed through this severe trial, he was released from his prison and led again to the temple.

For a second time his spiritual eyes were opened by the magic power of the Hierophant, and he was made to behold in his vision a *Griffin* and a *turning wheel with four spokes*. Then the whole process of Evolution became clear to his understanding, and he saw how in the course of millions of ages, worlds upon worlds had been evolved from the incomprehensible *centre*. He beheld waves of Life passing from planet to planet, and each fiery orb, each globe, each solar system, had peculiar forms of its own, and all these various forms were manifestations of one and the same Supreme Power, that men call "God," and formed out of its own substance.

The air, the earth, and the water were filled with forms of life, having bodies of a kind of matter too refined to be seen by mortal eyes. Some were luminous, others dark, and the regions above the sphere of the Earth were inhabited by beings of a seemingly supernatural beauty. He saw the *Nature-spirits* of the four elements. He saw what Man had been in the distant past and what he would be at a future period of time far beyond the calculation of mortals. He saw how the gross material elements of which the Earth is now composed, would in the far-distant future be changed into a substance of a superior and ethereal kind, so that what we now call "Earth" would be like water, and what we call "Water" like air, and what we call "Air" like the ether of space, and with the transformation of all things, Man himself would enter into a superior state of existence.

The science which deals with these problems is far too grand and extensive to be more than merely touched upon in these pages, nor would it benefit the uninitiated reader, if we were to enter into its details; for as long as the interior perception which enables men to perceive these things is not opened, such a discussion will be a mere matter of speculation, serving more for amusement than for the attainment of knowledge.

In this degree he was taught the great law of *Karma;* that is to say, the law of Cause and Effect, not merely upon the physical plane, where the law of *Mechanics* exists, but in that higher realm, where divine *Justice* rules supreme, where *Good* finds its own reward, and *Evil* its own punishment. He saw that whatever man may think or do, would produce a corresponding reaction upon himself, and that he who benefited others is thereby benefiting himself, while he who injures others is thereby decreeing his own punishment. He saw that the acts of men are the external symbols of their interior lives, and that every thought and act has a tendency to repeat itself. Thoughts seemed to him like beings struggling for life, seeking to become embodied in acts; and if they were once thus embodied, they clung to their life in the same way as man clings to his, but the power which invested these thoughts with life was the Will, and unless man's thoughts were kept alive by his

Will, they died and putrefied like the corporeal things upon the physical plane.

The password of this degree was *Heve*, and its understanding conveyed a knowledge of the bisexual nature of aboriginal Man.[1]

The length of time during which the *Necoris* had to remain in the second degree, before he was permitted to enter the third, called *Melanephores*, depended on his own progress. Many never attained any higher than the second degree; but those who were permitted to advance higher had to pass through the *Portal of Death;* for this was the name of the door through which they who desired to obtain powers which belong to a higher than merely personal existence had to enter, before they could acquire them.

Without hesitation Jehoshua followed those who were appointed to guide him. They descended into the tombs, where the mummies were kept and which were to be a living tomb to him, if he did not succeed in liberating himself therefrom by his own magic power. The room which he entered was filled with corpses of the dead, while in the midst of the chamber stood the sarcophagus of *Osiris* still overflowing with blood. The *Paraskites* — i.e. the men who opened the bodies of the dead — and the *Heroi* — who attended to the embalming — were at their work. From thence he entered into another room, where he was met by all the *Melanephores*, dressed in black. They took him before the *King*, and the latter,

---

[1] *Clem. Alexander*, In Protept.

addressing him in a very kind manner, advised him to desist from further attempts to penetrate still deeper into the mysteries, and to remain satisfied with that which he had already gained. He praised the Neophyte for his courage and virtues and told him that it were better for him now to remain contented and to desist from further research. He told him that if he would do so, he would be highly honored by all on account of the knowledge he had already gained; and in token of the high esteem in which he held the Neophyte, the king took his own golden crown from his head and offered it to him. But Jehoshua, understanding the meaning of this symbol, threw the crown down upon the floor and stepped upon it with his foot, saying that it was not his object to be admired and to gratify his ambition for fame or to be praised by men; but that he desired wisdom and desired it for its own sake alone.

As he did so, a cry of indignation arose from those present and a ceremony took place which upon the external plane represented the well-known internal truth, that [*Ambition* is the king of all passions and that to give up one's Ambition is like giving up one's own self; for man's soul being made up to a great extent of desires, dies the *mystic death*, when he kills his ruling desire.] It is then "as if the heart were bleeding and the whole life of man seems to be utterly dissolved."[1]

This was the terrible ordeal through which Jehoshua had to pass, and it is *the* ordeal through which every one

[1] *M. C.* "Light on the Path."

will have to pass, before he can enter the Temple of Wisdom.

Let not the reader suppose that we are describing a farce, such as may be seen enacted in some lodge of some modern "secret society." Whether the events described in these pages ever took place on the *external* or on the *internal* plane, or on *both*, the reader may decide for himself. If such things are enacted merely externally without taking place internally, then they are mere shams. (Every external act which is not a true representation of internal life is a sham, and our modern civilization is made up of such shams.) Our secret societies have come into possession of some of the forms and ceremonies used by the ancient Egyptians; but they have merely the *form;* the spirit went away long ago.

The judgment of the departed soul before *Pluto, Rhadamantes*, and *Minos* was then enacted; for when the king of *Ambition* in the soul of man dies, his daughter *Vanity* dies with him, and in its place arises a sense of one's unworthiness. The *accusing, judging*, and *revenging* angels then appear in the soul, until the tortured heart sends its despairing cries to the *Redeemer*, the *Truth;* when the celestial powers awaken within, to comfort the soul and guide her to the harbor of *Peace*.

During this process or ceremony the whole of Jehoshua's past life, with all the minutest details that ever took place within his mental organization, appeared before his vision; but when the initiation was ended, he knew that the lower elements within his soul had died and that he himself had been changed into another being. He then received the special instructions belonging to this degree, and he was especially shown the sanctity of all life and the full meaning of the words: "*Thou shalt not kill.*"

While he remained in this degree, the *hierogrammatical* art of writing, the history of Egypt, geography, cosmology, and astronomy were taught him; but his principal occupation, in this as in all other degrees, was the cultivation of the power of Intuition, by which man may know the truth and attain wisdom, independent of books or external information and without the necessity of adopting the opinions of others.

For a long time Jehoshua remained in tombs, attending to the disposal of the bodies of the dead; nor was any one of the members of this degree ever permitted to leave them during the rest of their natural lives, unless they attained that magic power, known to the *Adept*, by which the astral body of man may leave at will the prison house of terrestrial body. Those who were not able to acquire this power had to remain in their tombs, and their duty was to attend to the embalming and the burial of the dead.

Thus the souls of those who are incapable of entering a higher state of consciousness during their terrestrial lives, will have to remain within their living tombs of gross matter, overshadowed by the darkness of ignorance, engaged in ministering to that which is worthless and without eternal life, and to preserve from decay useless memories of terrestrial things. They will continue to follow their worthless occupations and be servants of empty forms and illusions until the angel of death releases them from their prisons, to lead them from the darkness of matter into the eternal darkness beyond.

THE HIGHER DEGREES.

He who thoroughly knows his own self, knows everything.

IN attempting to describe some of the mysteries of the higher degrees in the Egyptian Brotherhood, we are attempting to enter upon a field where only those can enter who have themselves obtained some experience of practical Occultism; for how could the *magic* processes that took place in the "*Battle of the Shadows*" be described to persons whose knowledge consists merely of the information they have received from an age which denies that magic or spiritual powers exist? It will require perhaps centuries of scientific investigation before our sceptics will understand the magic power of the *spiritually awakened Will*, and before they can be brought to a knowledge that feats of Magic do not belong to the realm of the fable, and it may require many centuries more, before such powers will become the property of the many.

Our age is the age of what is called "Reason," *i.e.* semi-animal Reason, not enlightened by Divine Wisdom, but drawing inferences from merely external things. It is ruled by those powers which are allegorically represented in the Bible by the "Pharisees and the Scribes," whose knowledge is based upon deductions drawn from the observation of illusive appearances, which they mistake for the Real, while the real is unknowable to them. In proportion as this fallible reasoning power has increased in strength, have men become unconscious of true Spirituality; that is to say, of the existence of a power to perceive spiritual and fundamental truths. With the loss of spiritual *knowledge* they have also lost the spiritual *Power* necessary to control the invisible spiritual forces. True *Gnostic* has become a thing of the past, *agnosticism* raises its head and boasts of its ignorance, and Science has become materialized so much that she can deal with nothing but the most gross and sensually perceptible things.

And yet the world is still full of Magic. The magic power of *Love* still exercises its influence over the hearts; the magic of *Imagination* still makes men mournful or glad; the *Will* of the strong still controls by its magic power the mind of the weak, and the foolish are still ruled by the superior magic power of the spirit of those who are wise; but such wonders like that of the growth of a tree, do not surprise us, merely because we are accustomed to witness them every day.

The Egyptian Adepts and Magicians may not have been in possession of all that our modern science knows in regard to the relations which exist between external phenomena; but they had a method, known only to few in our present age, to develop the power to look into that realm called the invisible, but which is a world far more real and substantial than the so-called visible world. Men are prone to jump at conclusions drawn from sensual observation and to regard the visible side of nature as the actual world and to reject that which is beyond sensual perception; but even a superficial reflection will convince man that the terms "visible" and "invisible" are merely *relative;* for whether or not a thing may be seen by us, depends not merely on its own nature, but also on the construction and quality of the organs of our perception. What may be seen by one, may be invisible to another who is devoid of the organ of sight; and what may be invisible to many, may be visible to those whose inner powers of perception have become open.

The fourth degree of the mysterious Brotherhood was called "*The Battle of the Shadows.*"[1] In this degree the *Christophores* — as he was now called — was taught the nature of *Good* and *Evil* and how to conquer Evil by Good. He was taught how to cut off the head of the beautiful *Gorgon*,[2] without hesitating on account of her almost supernaturally beautiful form. He was instructed in the art of *Necromancy, i.e.* the art to deal with the *astral bodies* of the dead and with those dangerous beings, called *Elementals*, who inhabit the *astral world*, and to make them subservient to their will. Woe to him whom the power of spiritual Will deserted even for one moment during these trials; the principles of Evil which he attempted to subject to his Will would

---

[1] *Tertullian*, " De Militis Corona."
[2] Medusa.

then become his masters, and insanity or death was the result.

(There is no relative Good without relative Evil. There is no man so pure, as not to have some animal elements within his constitution, and were there such a man, he would not be able to develop higher; for it is this very animal element from which the soul of man draws its nourishment and strength to rise higher and to become more spiritual. Not to destroy, but to make use of the elements of evil in man for the purpose of accomplishing good, is the object of the higher education. When the higher life begins to awaken within the soul and the light of the Spirit penetrates into the regions of the *Elementals*, these animal *Egos* begin to revolt and to rise to the surface. They may even appear in objective form and persecute their creator. Then the dread *Dweller of the Threshold* may show his face. He is nothing else but a product of man's own imagination, but nevertheless living and as real as any other living thing among the so-called realities of this world, and if the candidate for initiation is subject to fear, he may become his victim, for the Dweller of the Threshold will then again and with increased power take possession of his mind.

There is a region in the soul of man in which such Dwellers reside. In very degraded persons this region swarms with living, semi-developed or full-grown animal principles and subjective monstrosities of all kinds and under certain conditions, especially if the physical organism is weakened by disease, they may — so to say — step out of their centre, and assume an objective form, clothing themselves in the grosser elements of matter and becoming visible even to the external senses.[1]

But if the candidate in that holy Brotherhood succeeded in overcoming all these obstacles, he became a partaker of the *Demiurgos*[2] and in possession of absolute Truth.[3] The *bitter cup* which he was made to drink, caused him to rise above all earthly ills arising from his lower nature, and he received his daily food from the *King*.[4] His name was then entered into the *Book of Life*, and he became one of the *judges of the country*. His emblem was an *Owl*, representing *Isis*, the goddess of Nature; he was presented with a *palm leaf* and an *olive branch*, the emblems of *Peace*. The "password" of that degree was IOA,[5] and the understanding of its exoteric signification involved a knowledge of the creative principle in Nature. Henceforth he received his instructions from no man, but from the *Demiurgic Mind*.

He who had attained the degree of *Christophores* was entitled to apply to the *Demiurgos* for the still higher degree of *Balahate*. In this degree he was permitted

---

[1] Abundant evidence of such cases may be found in the *Acta Sanctorum*, although the accounts related therein are treated as fables even by the clergy, who cannot find a rational explanation for them. Modern Spiritualism furnishes similar examples.

[2] The creative power in nature.
[3] *Athenæus*, Lib. 9.
[4] *Diodorus Siculus*, Lib. i.
[5] Jehovah.

to see Typhoon[1] in his terrible form; of endless extent, containing within himself all that exists in the Universe; the All-creator and All-destroyer,

> "With eyes and faces, infinite in form,
>   The everlasting Cause, a mass of Light,
> In every region hard to look upon;
>   Bright as the blaze of burning fire and sun,
> On every side, and vast beyond all bounds."[2]

But the *Balahate* had awakened to a full consciousness of the immortal principle within, and was no longer terrified to see the destruction of all changeable things. He now knew the nature of the *Secret Fire* that regenerates the world and which renders him who comes into its possession immortal.

In the sixth degree the Adept was instructed by the Demiurgos in all the secrets of *Astrology;* that is to say, in the science of the spiritual aspects of the stars; he learned to know the directions of the spiritual life-currents, pervading the *Soul of the Universe;* he became even a being superior to the *Devas* and *Angels* and in possession of all spiritual powers.

The seventh and highest degree, called *Pancah*, could not be applied for, but was conferred by the power of divine *grace* upon those who were willing to receive it. In this divine degree, the holiest of holies, the ultimate mystery was revealed to the spiritual perception of the Adept. He received a *Cross*, which he had to wear

---

[1] Divinity.   [2] *I. Davies*, Bhagavad Gita, xi. 14.

continually during his terrestrial life,[1] the hair upon his head was cut off,[2] he received the key to the understanding of all the mysteries,[3] he obtained the privilege to elect the king of the country,[4] or — to speak in plain words and leave off allegorical expressions — his soul became one with the ruler of All, and he entered into the essence of God.

[1] *Rufius*, Lib. ii. Cap. 29.
[2] *Pierius*, Lib. 32.
[3] *Plutarch*, " De amore fraterno."
[4] *Synesus*, " De Providentia."

THE WISDOM RELIGION.

The inner laws of the universe can be known by studying the inner laws of that little world called " Man."

IT has not been ascertained how long Jehoshua Ben-Pandira remained in Egypt, nor what degrees he attained in the Holy Brotherhood; but it is believed that he underwent many of the severe trials to which those who desired to be initiated into the mysteries were subjected. He was taught many of these sublime secrets, or, to express it more correctly: As the bud of a Lotus flower gradually opens under the influence of the sunlight, so his mind opened to the understanding of the divine mysteries of the Wisdom Religion. He perceived that *God* had a spiritual and a material aspect; that He is all things, and that for this cause "He hath many names, because he is the One Father, and that He also hath no name, for He is the Father of All";[1]—that this one and universal *Father* had created the world in his own Mind, endowed it with His own Life, and thrown it into objectivity by His own Will.

He perceived and realized that this divine essence which caused the universe to take form and to grow, is the same that forms the corner-stone of the living tem-

---

[1] *Hermes Trismegistus*, V. 33.

ple of God, called *Man*, and that the essence constituting the foundation and the innermost centre of Man is in no way different from that of the universal God, and that therefore "earthly man is a little god in a mortal body, while the God of the Universe is an immortal self-existent Man."[1] He found no *death* in the universe, but a continual change of form, while the Life that causes these changes of form remains always the same. That which is imperfect has to be remodelled and to become perfect; but that which is perfect and therefore eternal requires no further change.

He saw that the whole of Nature is a thing of Life, subject — like all living beings — to periods of activity and rest; that after a *day* of activity, lasting perhaps for millions of ages, the great phantasmagoria constituting the universe ceases to be manifest, and is followed by a *night* of equal duration, during which all things exist in a subjective condition in the mind of the creator, until "God" again awakens from his slumber, to speak once more the divine command:

LET THERE BE LIGHT!

Then ends the night; the *mystic Sun* appears,
Filling all space with Life and Harmony,
With Consciousness and Sound. Again begins
The Wheel to turn, and the celestial Powers,
The Master-builders of the Universe,[2]
Whose work had ceased with the evening tide,
Begin again their labor. Glowing globes

[1] *Ibid.* IV. 193.   [2] The Dhyan Chohans.

Of radiant matter, luminous and bright,
Condense and clothe themselves in varied hues,
Evolving shells of rocks and precious stones.
And mother earth puts on her festive dress,
To bid a joyful welcome to her children.
Plants, animals, appear; at last comes *Man*,
The king, a spirit of ethereal shape,
Form'd of the essence that produces gods,
Surrounded by the paradise which God
Created in his sphere. He is the Lord
Of every living thing, the masterpiece
Of the constructor of the universe;
His substance is the Light, his thoughts divine,
His wisdom great, his happiness supreme.
Thus might he live eternally, in bliss
Unspeakable, communing with himself,
Unconscious of that lower sense of self,
Which causes isolation of the form.
But in the womb of Matter dwells desire,
The ancient tempter. Man averts his eyes
From his celestial source, and he begins
To sink into the darkness. Denser grows
And more compact his form, as he descends
To seek for knowledge in the realm of Matter.
Imprisoned in the form, his senses close
To the perception of celestial things,
And senses of a grosser kind appear,
Fit merely to behold the things of Earth,
For "where man's treasure is, there is his heart";
Uniting with the object he desires,
He shares its nature. The immortal soul
Combin'd with mortal clay is rendered mortal,
And mortal things transformed may rise up
Beyond the region of mortality.

Spirit is Life; but Matter has no life,
Which it may claim its own; the source of Life
Is that celestial Sun, invisible
To mortals, but eternal, self-existent
And glorious, in whose resplendent rays
All beings move and live, by whom we all
Exist, whose altar is the heart of Man.
This is the "Fall of Man" and the descent
Of the bright Spirit to the realms of darkness,
Occurring now as in those ancient times,
When Man was tempted by the mythic snake
For men are still attracted by desire,
Appearing in the beauteous form of lust,
Or in the shape of gold or love of fame,
Appealing to his sense of selfishness,
And thus degrading him, and many sink
To lower depths, while others rise again
By throwing off desire for earthly things,
And gaining knowledge of celestial truths
By bursting through the misty veil of matter
That hides them from the light.

       Desire to live
And to enjoy the pleasures of this life
Produces birth in living mortal forms;
Then follows life with all its sufferings,
Its evanescent joys, old age, and death,
And all the ills that follow those whose souls
Remain attach'd to matter; after this
Comes birth again, and thus the wheel revolves
Unceasingly.   But the celestial Sun
Of happiness continues to shine,
Sending his rays of love, of light, and life

Into the hearts of men and filling them
With longings for their former state of bliss.
And some perceive the light and hear the voice
Of wisdom speaking in their darkened souls,
Speaking to them: "O men! Let there be Light!"
And waking from their sleep they start and listen,
Like one awakening from some idle dream.
Some realize the presence of the Truth
Within their hearts and follow the Redeemer,
And throwing off that foolish love of self,
Their minds expand beyond the narrow limits
Of personality. Then can the prison house
Of flesh no longer hold the glorious spirit,
Which gained freedom from the love of self.

This is the history of man's redemption
Without a passport from a man-made priest.
The great Redeemer speaks to every man,
But many hear the voice and sink again
To sleep, preferring darkness to the light.

What is the cause of all our suffering,
But the desires that chain us to the flesh?
No one is free, but he who has outlived
All love of earthly things, all love of self.
What are the forms of life that please the eye,
But evanescent clouds? and what is man
In his corporeal form but air and dust?
He lords the earth to-day and feeds the worms
Of earth to-morrow. Who but God can claim
To be immortal? Therefore seek the God
Who speaks within thy heart, and say with him:
"Let there be Light!" — Seek for the light that shines
Within thy heart and learn to know thyself.
Learn to adore, and thou shalt find the Truth.

THE TEMPTATION.

There is no absolute evil. A house divided against itself would fall: an evil power, being evil in the absolute, would be evil in regard to itself and destroy itself. Evil is necessary to afford experience, and experience leads to ultimate good; but those who employ evil means to attain good results associate themselves with evil, and by creating evil will perish with it.

JEHOSHUA had attained in Egypt some of the lower degrees of Adeptship, when he was advised by his superiors to return to Palestine for the purpose of teaching the truth to his countrymen and to lift them up from their state of degradation and superstition; for practical occultism does not consist in merely leading a life of contemplation and virtue and attending to one's own spiritual culture. To do so would after all be only a refined state of selfishness. It is equally necessary to do external work; that is to say, to work for the benefit of others, to help to drive back the powers of darkness and ignorance, to assist in the work of ennobling mankind, and to raise it up to a higher level in the scale of evolution.

Such a work for others brings with it its own reward; for as it has been well said by one of the greatest thinkers and poets,[1] "A quiet life in a solitude is use-

[1] Schiller.

ful for the development of one's *talents;* but for the strengthening of the *character*, an active co-operation in the battle of Life is required."

Jehoshua had attained a high degree of that interior power of perception which enables man to hear the voice of divine *Inspiration* speak within the heart without any danger of misunderstanding. To accomplish this it is necessary not merely to become a master over one's evil desires, but also to keep the disorderly intellectual powers of the mind subject to the control of the Spirit, so that the Intellect may become our friend and servant, but cease to assume the place belonging to Divine Wisdom. The Intellect is easily influenced by the desires of the lower self, but Wisdom is above all selfish considerations; she recognizes no personal claims which are not in accordance with eternal Truth. The Intellect is changeable and mortal; Wisdom is eternal, unchangeable, and immortal. The Intellect can only become immortal by amalgamating with Wisdom. If the decisions of Wisdom and those of the Intellect are in harmony and identical with each other, then the mortal Intellect rises up to the state of immortal divine *Intelligence.*

Jehoshua returned to Palestine. His object was to convince his countrymen that God will only help those who help themselves, and that all external circumstances are the results of interior conditions; that if they desired to extricate themselves from their deplorable condition, they would have to call to their aid the divine power existing within themselves, instead of remaining indolent and expecting external help from a God such as they had created within their own imagination.

There were at the time of which we are writing a number of people in Galilee of more advanced thought than the rest. They were known as the *Nazarenes;* the majority of them were living on the east side of the river Jordan and in the vicinity of the lake Tiberias, and *John the Baptist* was their prophet. This man, originally of the priestly caste of the Levites, was looked upon by the Pharisees as being a renegade to their order, because his doctrines did not conform to their orthodox views. He had resigned his sacerdotal office at the temple, with all its emoluments, and chosen a life of poverty. Clad in rough skins, his noble face almost hidden by his shaggy hair and flowing beard, his appearance was awe-inspiring, and his voice was strong, re-echoing in the hearts of men like the sound of thunder that reverberates through the mountains.

"Repent!" he cried; "the day of judgment is near. Listen no longer to the seductions of sensual life, but seek the divine life within you. I do not ask you to give up the pleasures of life for the purpose of becoming misanthropes, but to realize that there is something far higher than merely animal pleasures or erroneous speculations; and if you rise up to the higher regions of thought and learn to know your own higher nature, sensual things will lose their attraction for you, and you will renounce them as worthless objects in the same sense as a grown-up man renounces the toys with which he used to play when a child, and for which he has no further use. I baptize you with the water of truth by directing your thoughts to that which is eternal; but the understanding I cannot give, for that must come from Wisdom, which is greater than Reason. First comes thought, and afterwards comes that interior *Illumination* by which men are baptized with *Fire* from the Holy Spirit of Truth, that descends upon those who are pure in heart, like a white dove descending from heaven. Man may be led up to the truth by argumentation, but he can only be saved by knowledge. Reason is the prophet, but Wisdom is the Redeemer. Thought must precede knowledge; but without the light of divine Wisdom thought is like a voice in the wilderness, calling for help; an intellect without Love becomes easily lost in the mazes of speculations and misleading opinions. Therefore you, who desire to be saved, repent of your errors; give up your selfishness, that causes you to seek for knowledge merely on account of the benefits you hope to derive therefrom; open your eyes to see the true saviour, the light of Wisdom, which you may find below the dark clouds of ignorance by which your heart is surrounded."

The fame of John the Baptist had spread all over the country; even the embodiment of selfishness, the great king *Herodes*, had heard his voice that sounded like the roar of a lion. This man, being a great profligate and entirely attracted by sensual pleasures, would not listen to the warning voice of Reason, but at the same time he was a great coward. He was afraid that what John the Baptist said might be true, after all. He did what the majority of men do at this day when their reason comes in conflict with their desires. He refused to listen to John the Baptist; he had him arrested and put into a prison, so that he might not be disturbed by his voice, and be left in the undisturbed enjoyment of the beautiful Herodias.

For some time Jehoshua remained with this prophet of the desert and his disciples. He taught them some of the truths he had learned in Egypt from the books of *Hermes Trismegistus*, called in Egypt *Meti*,[1] and his companions wrote down some of the fragments he taught, and these fragments were afterwards transmitted to their successors.

After the imprisonment of John the Baptist, Jehoshua retired for a while into the wilderness, to devote himself to meditation and self-examination. There are moments in the life of every man when he feels the necessity to retire within himself and to look into his own interior soul. If he succeeds in locking the door of the chamber of his mind against all sensual thoughts that may arise from external influences, to keep the wandering thoughts steady, "as a lamp sheltered from the wind does not flicker," to plunge down into the

[1] The Gospel according to Matthew.

mysterious depths of his own innermost being, then may he find the Divinity within his own soul.

Let not this be called a fancy. Useless would it be for a man who has not found his own higher self, to imagine that he found it and to believe himself to be a god. Such an assumption would be sure to bring on his perdition. If the internal god reveals himself to man, he does so in a manner which leaves no room for doubt; but which must be experienced before it can be known, and which can therefore not be revealed to those who refuse to receive him.

There are vast solitudes in Judea, where the blazing sun sends his rays into the treeless desert. There nothing is to be seen but bare rocks and loose stones filling the dried-up beds of the creeks, wherein during the rainy season water collects, but where during the rest of the year no moisture is found. No life is there, except perhaps a snake gliding over the sand and an eagle floating high up in the air watching his prey; the heated air scorches the parched lips, and all around is desolation and death, while overhead expands the sky, the emblem of Infinity.

There are solitudes within the human soul, to which man may retire. There are deserts where nothing is to be seen but a jumble of adopted opinions and theological doctrines, and where reason looks in vain for a drop of the water of truth. Sometimes lakes and rivers appear at a distance; but as we approach, that which appeared to be true proves to be merely a mirage, a work of delusion. Things that look in the moonlight of external reason like precious fruits or like jewels and pearls are often found upon examination in the sunlight of Wisdom to be nothing but worthless rubbish. Over our head shines the sun of Truth in the infinite realm, while in the dark caverns of the soul lurk the snakes of evil desires.

To some such desert Jehoshua retired, and there he fought once more the great battle with his own self. He looked within his soul and he found therein reflected the condition of mankind; for (man is an integral part of Humanity, and in proportion as we learn to know our own soul we lose all sense of separateness and realize that we are one with all mankind; we are in humanity, and humanity is within ourselves.) As he looked in that *magic mirror*, — the Soul, — he saw therein reflected the images of all the miseries produced by ignorance, and the ardent desire arose in his heart to save mankind from error; to kill the monster of darkness, to destroy once again the golden calf of self-adulation, and to restore the worship of the Spirit of Wisdom, whose temple is in the soul. While he thought of becoming a saviour to mankind, the sense of the "*I*" arose in his consciousness, and the tempter approached him in the shape of *Ambition*, the king of all the powers of evil.

"Powerful one," whispered the tempter, "if thou wilt save mankind, *cause these stones to become bread*, enable men to employ Intelligence for base purposes;

for they will care little for spiritual truths unless they can make them serve some temporal purpose. Their material necessities are nearer to them than the things of whose existence they know nothing, or whether they be at all useful to them. Men do not care for the truth; they only care for the material benefits which may result from its knowledge. Go and improve the material condition of mankind. Teach them how to make gold and to gain easily comfort and luxury. Then, when their terrestrial wants are provided for, will they find time to attend to their spiritual salvation. Go and teach them the hidden secrets of nature, so that they may kill their enemies and acquire riches. Feed the hungry and save them the trouble of working, liberate those who are slaves and too indolent to help themselves, and thou wilt be worshipped by all."

But Jehoshua, rising above the plane of selfishness, repulsed the evil one, and said: "Material wealth and comfort is not all that mankind requires; their spiritual condition is of far greater importance than temporal benefits given to them without their own efforts. The power for good can only grow by a constant battle with evil. It is well that man should learn all the external conditions by which he is surrounded, but every gratification of his selfish desires only calls into existence a legion of other desires and fastens still stronger the links by which he is chained to Matter. 'Evil' is as much a necessary element in the process of evolution as 'good,' for the only way to freedom is through suffering; only he who has fought in the battle can come out victorious."

"But," answered the evil one, "how wilt thou convince mankind that this terrestrial world is merely a world of illusions, and that there is a higher state of existence? If thou couldst perform wonders and miracles, they would perhaps be willing to believe. *Cast thyself down from the pinnacle of Jerusalem*, degrade thyself by descending to the plane of the intellectual understanding, and men will believe in thee. Men do not love the divine truth, because they do not know it; and before they will seek to know it, they must be made to believe that it exists. If thou canst make its existence plausible by performing some wonderful feats, then will they be willing to make a bargain and to exchange terrestrial baubles for celestial treasures. Does not the light eternally shine into darkness, and does the darkness believe that it exists?"

To this the Higher Self of Jehoshua replied: "Divine Wisdom belongs to the realm of Light, and cannot descend to the intellectual comprehension of mortals; those who seek for the truth must themselves rise up to its understanding.[1] Men must come up to divine wisdom; it cannot descend to their level. Moreover, it is not a mere *belief* in the truth, which will save mankind;

---

[1] When the truth was brought before the judgment seat of the intellect, and requested to prove intellectually his claims, "he never answered him a word; insomuch that the governor (of the mind) marvelled greatly." — Matthew xxvii. 12.

they should have their own knowledge. Those who cannot have faith without external evidence, are not in the possession of knowledge. Let them open their eyes for the perception of spiritual things and cease to cling to adopted beliefs. Let them seek for the truth within themselves, and not within the opinions of another."

"Wilt thou, then," said the demon of Self, "take away the crutches with which poor Humanity hobbles along? Wilt thou destroy her toys and awaken her from the peaceful slumber in which she finds repose? Dost thou know what will be the consequences of such a rash act? Men do not wish to be free from creeds and opinions, for they possess no knowledge. They hate freedom, and prefer to cling to the slavery of their creeds. They do not want to be their own masters, but they must have some one to obey. If thou destroyest their favorite creed to-day, they will have another one to-morrow. What should they do without a creed? They are afraid to think for themselves; they must have some man to think for them. Thou wilt make them free, but thou shalt not succeed. Fasten their chains, and they will be happy. Give them a herdsman to follow, and they will be contented. Give them somebody to obey. Give them by all means an *Authority* in which they may believe. Behold, I am the *Devil of Self;* my kingdom extends all over the world. *Fall down and sacrifice thy dignity to me*, enter my being, appeal to men's love of self, and you will be the ruler of the world."

As he spoke these words, the demon expanded in size,

and his body, like an immense cloud of darkness, seemed to extend all over the surface of the earth, and Jehoshua saw that the thoughts and actions of the vast majority of men and women upon this globe were all ruled by selfishness. There were almost none to be found who loved Divine Wisdom for her own sake, while all the rest merely pretended to love her, because they expected favors from her. They loved the Truth merely on account of the benefits that might be derived from its knowledge here or in the hereafter, and thus they did not love Divine Wisdom, but merely her gifts. Not being able to know the Truth, because they were not attracted to it by an unselfish love for Divine Wisdom, they were satisfied with anything, however false, which was represented to them as being the truth, and thus they worshipped their own idols. But there were a few who actually loved the truth for its own sake, and they appeared like luminous stars within that dark mass of ignorance.

But as Jehoshua looked still deeper into the hearts of men, he found that this love of self was merely a property of the surface of the shell of which men are composed, and that there was, after all, a germ of genuine love of the truth contained within the depths of every human heart. If this germ could be developed and brought to the surface, and the love of self be made to occupy a *back-seat*, then would the love for absolute Good come *to the front*, and men would learn to know the Truth. The love of self is inherent in human nature, and it cannot be entirely suppressed as long as men live in corporeal forms ; but it can be made to appear as a matter of secondary consideration, while an unselfish attendance to duty should be a matter of the greatest importance to all.

Therefore the Divinity of Jehoshua arose to the surface, and said to the Demon of Self: "*Get thee behind me, Satan!*" and as he spoke these words, the demon shrank into minute proportions and disappeared from sight, and a flood of light entered the soul of Jehoshua. He now became fully conscious that he had entered a new state of existence ; an interior *Illumination* took place, and he saw that his personality was not his real self, but merely an instrument which he had created for the purpose of fulfilling a mission upon this Earth. He had now gained a great victory over his own illusive self and entered into the sanctuary of the Temple of Truth.

THE SERMON UPON THE MOUNT.

The Truth teaches nothing else but its own existence; it is for Man to rise up to that height where he may arrive at its understanding.

JEHOSHUA had now become strong; he had become a prophet and Adept. Before his interior Illumination took place, he had not known that firm conviction which he possessed now. He had perceived the power of the spirit like a blind man, who feels the heat of the sunshine without being able to see the light; but now he had gained true knowledge, he had become acquainted with his *Bride, Divine Wisdom;* and when during his sermons, being carried away by his aspirations for Truth, he rose into the regions of divine thought to embrace her, his human nature was lost to all consciousness of personal limited existence; his *Bride* took form in him, and it was no more the man Jehoshua who spoke divinely inspired words; but it was Divine Wisdom herself that spoke through his lips. His whole being appeared on such occasions to be permeated by the Light of the *Logos;* yea, for all we know, it may have been the *Logos* itself manifesting through him.

This may explain why, like the Avatars of old, he

spoke of himself as being *The Christ, The Truth*, and *The Son of God*. This Spirit of Wisdom, that in ancient times had spoken through the mouth of *Krishna*, saying: "I am the way, the supporter, lord, witness, abode, and friend;"[1] "I am the beginning, the middle and the end of all existing things,"[2] repeated these words through the lips of Jehoshua, saying: "I am the way, the truth, and the life.[3] . . . I am the Alpha and Omega; the beginning and the end";[4] and this divine spirit still continues to speak in the same manner in the heart of every one who is able to rise above the Sphere of Self and to become for the time being one with his God.

He taught in many of the towns and villages of Galilee, and gained the hearts of the people by his great beauty and eloquence and by that power which always inspires those who are firmly convinced that they are teaching the truth. From village to village he went, preaching anew the old gospel of fraternal love; and many times when the doors of the synagogues were closed against him, he may have been seen, standing upon a hill, surrounded by the listening crowd, while the evening breeze played with his long flowing locks, and above him on the distant sky shone that bright constellation of stars called the *Southern Cross*, as if it were to reveal the future that was waiting for him — a cross upon this Earth and eternal glory in Heaven.

[1] Bhagavad Gita, ix. 13.
[2] *Ibid*, x. 20.
[3] John xiv. 6.
[4] Revelation i. 8.

Those few and rare persons, the *regenerated* ones in the spirit, in whom the *Word* has become alive, and through whom Divine Wisdom manifests itself, require no preparation for their speeches, nor any elaborate arrangement for their ideas; because it is not their own systems and opinions which they present to their audiences; but it is the Truth itself, expressing itself through them. We are not now referring to those who speak in a trance, or as if controlled by a superior spirit, nor to those who talk of whatever enters their brain; but to those who travel the road to Adeptship, who are able to hear the eternal *Word* in their hearts, speaking to them with no uncertain sound, and who give it external expression. Thus the bird requires no instructor to know what melody to sing, and in moments of joy or grief, when Nature pours forth her own sentiments, without hypocrisy and without restraint, thoughts rise from the heart to the lips and become words, as the waters of a well rise to the surface without preparation and without artifice — being doubly powerful from being produced by nature.

His words coming as they did, — not from the brain, but from the heart, — went to the hearts of the hearers; being in possession of the truth, " he taught as one having authority, and not as the scribes," [5] who repeat what they have learned in books, without being themselves convinced of the truth of their doctrines, nor inclined to follow the rules which they prescribe for others.

[5] Matthew vii. 29.

Thus we find him one evening upon the *Mount*, in the midst of his followers, teaching them ancient truths in beautiful allegorical forms, which were understood by his hearers, because the truth was with them; but which are not understood by our theologians, because the truth is not with them. Having departed from our modern civilization, having been driven away by clericalism, priestcraft, and external reasoning, crucified and killed by our modern "Pharisees and scribes," the truth has departed from our religious systems, and the allegories of the Bible are not understood, but accepted merely in their external literal meaning, thus degrading Divine Wisdom into mere rubbish. Let us invoke the spirit of *Common Sense* to enlighten our mind and to explain to us to a certain extent the esoteric meaning of a few of the doctrines taught by Jehoshua upon the *Mount*. We well know that many words will be required to bring within the grasp of the intellect truths which can be imparted by a few allegories to the wise, and we also know that the explanations given below do not exclude other explanations equally true.

MATTHEW, CHAPTER V.

1. And seeing the multitude, he went up into a mountain, and when he was set, his disciples came unto him.

    Divine Wisdom being aware of a great multitude of intellectual powers in the mind, desiring knowledge, went with them into the mountain of Faith, and when tranquillity of the mind was established, the organs for intuition became opened.

2. And he opened his mouth and taught them, saying:—

Then the Spirit of Divine Wisdom came to the consciousness of the mind, and said:—

3. "Blessed are the poor in spirit, for theirs is the kingdom of heaven."

Happy are those, whose heads are not full of idle speculations, opinions, and theories, but who are able to receive the truth in its purity, as it comes from the source of all wisdom, being reflected in their minds, like the image of a ship sailing upon a tranquil lake is mirrored in the water. Happy are those who listen to the voice of their conscience and see by the light of their intuition without attempting to pervert by the sophistry of their external reasoning the truths which they intuitionally perceive.

4. "Blessed are they that mourn, for they shall be comforted."

Blessed are those who do not seek for happiness in terrestrial illusions, but recognize the reality of the ideal world. Their mortal forms may suffer, but by rising mentally to a higher state of consciousness above personality and limitation, they will be comforted.

5. "Blessed are the meek, for they shall inherit the Earth."

Happy are those who have no personal desires, for they are already in possession of all things. What could be offered to increase the happiness of one who is already perfectly happy and who has no ambition to gratify?

6. "Blessed are they which do hunger and thirst after righteousness, for they shall be filled."

Blessed are they who love the truth for its own sake, for by their aspirations they will rise up to its understanding.

7. "Blessed are the merciful, for they shall obtain mercy."

Those whose hearts are full of love and benevolence for all, will attract the love of all others.

8. "Blessed are the pure in heart, for they shall see God."

Only in a pure and tranquil soul can the image of Divine Wisdom be reflected and be recognized by the mind without any distortions.

9. "Blessed are the peacemakers, for they shall be called the children of God."

The peacemakers in the mind of man are those spiritual elements which raise him above the sphere of limitation and personality and attract him to the Eternal. Being of a divine nature, they are properly called the children of God.

10. "Blessed are they which are persecuted for righteousness' sake, for theirs is the kingdom of heaven."

Power grows by resistance. Those who overcome temptations and remain true to their spiritual *faith*, even if they suffer for it, will become stronger in knowledge and in the happiness resulting therefrom.

11 and 12. "Blessed are ye, when men shall revile you, and persecute you, and shall say all manner of evil against you falsely, for my sake. Rejoice and be exceeding glad, for great is your reward in heaven: for so persecuted they the prophets which were before you."

Such an appeal to the vanity, selfishness, and ambition of men and to their hope for reward, asking them to rejoice over lies and over the ignorance of others, cannot be anything else but a pious interpolation, unless it refers to a certain occult process, during which the lower elemental powers in man become rebellious, when they feel the approach of the truth, and they then begin to revile him.

13. "Ye are the *Salt* of the earth, but if the Salt have lost its savor, wherewith shall it be salted? It is thence good for nothing, but to be cast out and trodden under foot of man."

The *Will* is the life of the soul; but if the Will becomes evil and loses its sanctity, the whole constitution of man will become evil and useless for good. Evil desires will arise which must be "trodden under foot" and overcome by virtue.

14. "Ye are the light of the world. A city that is set on the hill cannot be hid."

The intelligent powers of men who have acquired wisdom, illumine the mind. Wisdom is self-evident to those who are wise, and even the inferior powers will recognize its beauty.

15. "Neither do men light a candle and put it under a bushel, but on a candle-stick, and it giveth light to all that are in the house."

The Wisdom should not be overshadowed by selfish desires. When the mind rises up to the sphere of wisdom, all its powers will become illumined by it.

16. "Let your light so shine before men, that they may see your good works and glorify your Father which is in heaven."

Do not merely talk, but *act* according to wisdom, and all the intelligent powers within and without you will then recognize the wisdom from which your actions arise, and rejoice over it.

17. "Think not that I am come to destroy the Law or the prophets. I am not come to destroy, but to fulfil."

A knowledge of the truth cannot cause men to act against divine law, but it will enable them to obey it. It is the misunderstanding and ignoring of the truth and the misinterpretation of the letter of the law, that causes men to disobey the law.

18. "For verily I say unto you: Till heaven and earth pass, one jot or one tittle shall in no wise pass from the law, till all be fulfilled."

The divine law of *Karma* will exist as long as the world exists. It is unchangeable. Prayers without acts avail nothing, for no favors are granted. The true way to pray is to rise up to a higher condition and to become ennobled in character by acting according to the unwritten law. Miracles are impossibilities. If even the least deviation of the Law of Evolution from its course were to occur, its eternal and unchangeable character would be forever destroyed.

19. "Whosoever, therefore, shall break one of these least commandments, and shall teach men so, he shall be called the least in the kingdom of heaven; but whoever shall do and teach them, the same shall be called great in the kingdom of heaven."

He who acts according to his own will and against the universal Will of God, loses the consciousness of his divine state, and lives in that of his narrow self; but he who acts according to the universal Law rises to its level, and his consciousness expands beyond the limits of personality, partaking of the nature of the divine mind.

20. "For I say unto you: that except your righteousness shall exceed the righteousness of the scribes and Pharisees, ye shall in no case enter the kingdom of heaven."

If you act merely according to the dictates of your external reasoning, and not from a direct spiritual perception of the truth, you are then not in that state of spiritual consciousness which constitutes the divine state of man. No one will enter heaven by argumentation.

21. "Ye have heard it was said by them of olden time: Thou shalt not kill, and whosoever shall kill shall be in danger of judgment."

As long as men are not capable of rising up to a perception of the truth, they may desist from evil deeds merely on account of the evil consequences that are believed to follow.

22. "But I say unto you: that whosoever is angry with his brother, shall be in danger of judgment."

But when you attain spiritual knowledge, you will know that it is your own state of mind and your thoughts, on which your future happiness depends; for the inner life of man is his real life; his external acts are merely the shadows of his thoughts. External acts produce effects upon the external plane; but man's thoughts and his will determine the condition of his inner life, and produce lasting effects upon that plane where he will exist when he re-enters the subjective state.

The above examples may be sufficient to show that the allegories of the Bible may be explained in a manner very different from that given by those who imagine that they are the Salt of the Earth and the Light of the World.

The inherent power of the truths which Jehoshua taught, his noble appearance, natural dignity, and kindness of manner gained for him the hearts of the people. On account of the mixed population of Galilee, bigotry and othodoxy were less prevalent there than in Judea. There were many "heathen" who had no religious prejudices, and even among the Jews there were not a few who had honest doubts in regard to the orthodox creed. The coming of the Redeemer who was to be their king and to drive the foreigners out of the country had been often heralded, and as often were they disappointed in their expectations. Jehoshua made no such claims. He wanted to improve the spiritual condition of the people; an improvement of their external condition would then be the natural consequence. Many recognized in him a man of advanced ideas, and he gained many followers among the inhabitants of that country.

There was, moreover, another circumstance which served to increase his popularity. It is well known to every Occultist that a certain degree of spiritual development is always accompanied by the development of certain occult powers, especially the power to heal diseases by the touch or by a mere exercise of the will, and also the power of reading intuitively the thoughts of others. Such things are not due to the action of any unnatural or supernatural cause; for the power of the Will and the principle of Life are said to be fundamentally identical, and he who can control his own Will becomes thereby able to direct the currents of Life within his own organism, and to transfer them upon others for the purpose of giving health and strength to them. It is likewise believed that those who have obtained the power to control their own thoughts and to steady their minds, may thereby become able to read the thoughts of others, because the mental images created by the latter become reflected and mirrored in the minds of those whose souls are tranquil, and such images may enter their consciousness.

Such powers Jehoshua possessed; he read the thoughts of the people, and knew their condition; and many a case of illness that was considered incurable by ordinary means of treatment was cured by the power of his *virtue*. As his fame spread, many sick persons were brought to him; he became a healer of the body as well as of the mind; he infused life in the bodies of his followers, and, dispelling the clouds of ignorance, he caused them to open their hearts to the influence of the divine light of the Truth. Thus he travelled through Galilee and Judea, and blessings followed in his path.

THE DOCTRINES OF THE CHRIST SPIRIT.

There is only one absolute Truth. Being universal, it is seen alike by all who are able to perceive it.

EVER since the most ancient times *Divine Wisdom* has taught the same doctrines through the mouths of the wise. Hermes Trismegistus, Confucius and Zoroaster, Buddha and Jehoshua, Plato and Socrates, Saint Martin and Jacob Boehmen, Theophrastus Paracelsus and Cornelius Agrippa, Shakespeare and Shopenhauer, and innumerable others have taught the same truths more or less complete, and each of these teachers clothed them in a form most suitable to his own understanding or adapted to the comprehension of his disciples.

For the sake of illustration, we will take a few examples from ancient books that existed before the Christian era; namely, the Bhagavad Gita, the books of Hermes Trismegistus, the Dhammapada of the Buddhists, and add corresponding verses of the Christian Bible, to show the similarity of these doctrines.

I. 1. "The wise man, ever devout, who worships the One, is the most excellent; for I am dear above all things to the wise man, and he is dear to me."— *Bhagavad Gita*, VII. 17.

2. "Embrace me with thy whole heart and mind, and whatsoever thou wouldst learn, I will teach thee."— *Hermes Trismegistus*, II. 3.

3. "He who reflects and meditates receives ample joy." — *Dhammapada*.

4. "Thou shalt love the Lord thy God with all thy heart, with all thy mind, and with all thy soul." — *Matthew*, XXII. 37.

II. 1. "I (Brahm) was never non-existent, nor thou, nor those rulers of men, nor shall any of us hereafter cease to be." — *Bh. Gita*, II. 12.

2. "I am that Light, the Mind, thy God, who am before the moist nature that appeared out of darkness, and that bright lightful *Word* is the Son of God." — *Hermes*, II. 8.

3. "He who has traversed this hazy and imperious world and its vanity, who is through and has reached the other shore, is thoughtful, guileless, free from doubts, free from attachment, and content, — him I call indeed a Brahmana." — *Dhamm*.

4. "Before Abraham was, I am." — *John*, VIII. 58.

III. 1. "He that spread out this All can never perish. No one is able to cause the destruction of the Eternal." — *Bh. Gita*, II. 17.

2. "What is God? Immutable and unalterable Good." — *Hermes*, I. 22. "God and the Father is Light and Life of which Man is made. If, therefore, thou learn and know thyself to be of the Life and Light, thou shalt again pass into the Life." — *Hermes*, II. 50.

3. "He who takes refuge with the (eternal) Law is delivered from all pain." — *Dhamm*.

4. "Heaven and earth shall pass away, but my *Word* (power) shall not pass away." — *Luke*, XXI. 33.

IV. 1. "As a man, having cast off his old garments, takes others that are new, so the embodied soul, having cast off the old bodies, enters into others that are new." — *Bh. Gita*, II. 22.

2. "That which is unchangeable is eternal, that which is always made is always corrupted." — *Hermes*, II. 22, 23.

3. "He who knoweth that this body is like froth and has learned that it is as unsubstantial as a mirage, will break the flower-pointed arrow of *Mara* and never see the king of death." — *Dhamm*.

4. "That which is born of the flesh is flesh, and that which is born of the Spirit is Spirit." — *John*, III. 6.

V. 1. "This embodied (soul) in the body of every one, oh son of Bharata! is ever indestructible, wherefore thou oughtest not to mourn for any living thing." — *Bh. Gita*, II. 30.

2. "Of the soul that part which is sensible is mortal, but that part which is governed by reason is immortal." — *Hermes*, I. 37. "Man is mortal because of his body, and immortal because of the substantial Man." — *Hermes*, II. 26.

3. "Happy is the arising of the Awakened. Even the gods envy those who are awakened." — *Dhamm*.

4. "I live, but not I, but Christ lived in me." — *Gal*. II. 20. "He that hath the Christ (in him) hath life, and he that hath not the Son of God hath no life." — 1 *John*, V. 22.

VI. 1. "A flowery kind of language is spoken by the unwise, who pride themselves in Veda words (in false reasoning and superficial logic), whose souls are full of lust, who regard (a sensual) heaven as the highest good. . . . The doctrines of these men, whose minds are carried away by mere words, are not formed for meditation." — *Bh. Gita*, II. 42.

2. "Terrestrial things do profit nothing the things of heaven; but celestial things profit all things upon the earth." — *Hermes*, I. 72. "To the foolish and evil, wicked and vicious, covetous, murderous, and profane, I am far off, giving place to the avenging demons." — *Hermes*, II. 56.

THE DOCTRINES OF THE CHRIST SPIRIT. 121

3. "Men driven by fear go to many a refuge, to mountains and forests, to groves and sacred trees, but that is not a safe refuge. . . . The thoughtless man, even if he can recite a long portion of the law (prayer), but is not a doer of it, has no part in the priesthood, but is like a cowherd, counting the cows of others." — *Dhamm.*

4. "Not every one that saith, Lord, Lord, shall enter the kingdom of heaven, but he that doeth the will of my Father which is in heaven." — *Matt.* VII. 21. "This people honoreth me with their lips, but their heart is far from me." — *Mark*, VII. 6.

VII. 1. "Neither intelligence nor self-possession belongs to the undevout man. There is no peace for him who is not self-possessed, and without peace how can there be happiness?" — *Bh. Gita*, II. 66.

2. "He that through error of Love loveth the body, abideth wandering in darkness, sensible, suffering the things of death." — *Hermes*, II. 40.

3. "Fools of little understanding have themselves for their greatest enemies, for they do deeds which must bear bitter fruits." — *Dhamm.*

4. "Except a man be born again, he cannot see the kingdom of God." — *John*, III. 13.

VIII. 1. "Brahma is the oblation, Brahma is the sacrificial butter, Brahma is the fire, the burnt offering is by Brahma. Into Brahma will he enter who meditates on Brahma in his work." — *Bh. Gita*, IV. 62.

2. "The like always takes to itself that which is like; but the unlike never agrees with the unlike." — *Hermes*, I. 84.

"That which in thee seeth and heareth, the Word of the Lord and the Mind, the Father God, differ not from one another and the union of these is life." — *Hermes*, II. 19.

3. "Without (spiritual) knowledge there is no meditation; without meditation there is no knowledge. He who has meditation and knowledge is near to *Nirvana*." — *Dhamm.*

4. "He that abideth in me and I in him, the same bringeth forth much fruit, for without me ye can do nothing." — *John*, XV. 5. "Whoso eateth (aspires) my (spiritual) flesh (substance) and drinketh (absorbeth) my blood (my power) dwelleth in me and I in him." — *John*, VI. 56.

IX. 1. "Let the Yogin constantly practise devotion, fixed in a secluded spot alone, having thought and self subdued . . . thinking on Me, intent on Me." — *Bh. Gita*, VI. 10.

2. "Depart from that dark light, be partakers of immortality, and leave or forsake corruption." — *Hermes*, II. 78. "Why have you delivered yourselves over unto death, having power to partake of immortality?" "O ye people, men born and made of the earth, which have given yourselves up to drunkenness and sleep and to the ignorance of Good, be sober and cease your surfeit, whereunto you are allured and visited by brutish and unreasonable sleep." — *Hermes*, II. 75.

3. "The disciples of Gautama are always well awake, and their thoughts day and night are always set on Buddha. Like a well-guarded fortress with defences within and without, so let a man guard himself. Not a moment should escape, for they who allow the right moment to pass suffer pain." — *Dhamm.*

4. "When thou prayest (meditatest), enter into thy closet (thy soul), and when thou hast shut the door (of the external senses), pray to the Father, which is in secret." — *Math.* VI. 6. "Watch and pray, that you may not enter into temptation." — *Math.* XXVI. 41.

X. 1. "He who sees Me everywhere and everything in Me, him I forsake not, and he forsakes not Me." — *Bh. Gita*, VI. 30.

2. "Shining steadfastly upon and around the whole mind, it enlightened all the soul, and loosing it from the bodily senses and motions, it draweth it from the body and changed it wholly into the essence of God. For it is possible, o Son, to be deified while yet it lodgeth in the body of man, if it contemplate the beauty of Good." — *Hermes*, IV. 18.

3. "Self is the lord of self; who else could be the Lord? With (the lower) self well subdued, a man finds a lord such as few can find." — *Dhamm.*

4. "That they all may be one, as thou, Father, art in me, and I in thee, that they also may be one in us." — *John*, XVII. 21.

XI. 1. "I am the source of all things; the whole (universe) proceed from Me. Thinking thus, the wise, who share my nature, worship Me." — *Bh. Gita*, X. 8.

2. "The glory of all things, God, and that which is divine, and the divine Nature, the beginning of things that are." — *Hermes*, III. 1.

3. "All that we are is the result of what we have thought; it is made up of our thoughts." — *Dhamm.*

4. "All things were made by Him, and without Him was not anything made. In Him was (*is*) the life, and the life was (*is*) the light of men." — *John*, I. 3.

XII. 1. "He who is the same to friend or foe . . . to whom pain and blame are equal; who is silent, content with every fortune, steadfast in mind, and worships Me, that man is dear to Me." — *Bh. Gita.*

2. "The strife of piety is to know God and to injure no Man, and in this way it becomes Mind. Such a soul, being pious and religious, is angelic and divine. After it is departed from the body, having striven for piety, it becomes the Mind or God." — *Hermes*, IV. 64.

3. "Let us live happily, not hating those who hate us; let us dwell free from hatred among men who hate us. Let a man overcome anger by love, evil by good, the greedy by liberality, the liar by truth." — *Dhamm.*

4. "Love your enemies; bless them that curse you, do good to them that hate you, and pray for them that persecute you." — *Math.* V. 40.

The above examples, *if their esoteric meaning is compared*, will be sufficient to show the great resemblance between the doctrines of the "New Testament" and those of the Eastern sages. But the circumstance that they refer to the same fundamental truths is by no means an indication that the writers have plagiarized each other.

The truth exists; it is as free as the air to all who are able to grasp it; it can neither be invented nor monopolized by man. Men may grasp and remodel ideas, and express them in new forms; but the truth is one and universal; it may be seen and described in one part of this globe as well as in another; it is eternal and does not change; and the doctrines it teaches through the mouths of those whose minds are illumined by wisdom, a million of years hence, will be the same which it taught a million of years ago. These doctrines *The Spirit of Christ* still teaches to those who will listen to him; for he is not dead, but lives as an immortal power whose name is *Divine Wisdom*, "*The Word*."

HERODIAS.

That which is said to have taken place in the history of the Jews is taking place to-day. Continually does Desire, to which Man is wedded, seek to alienate him from Reason, and by appealing to Passion she often succeeds in his destruction.

GAY was the throng which crowded the halls at the fortress of Makur, where the birthday of *Herodes the Great* was to be celebrated. Stately soldiers with glittering armors and helmets, beautiful ladies clad in rich garments and adorned with their most precious jewels, filled the rooms; Nubian and Arabian servants were seen hastening through the corridors; the walls were adorned with costly hangings and with an abundance of garlands and flowers, to prepare for the banquet, for a great orgy was to take place in that castle, to please the great king; while in its subterranean dungeons languished the prophet John the Baptist. Let us throw a glance at the supposed history of those times.

Herodes Antipas, the king of Judea, was an object of hate and fear to the Jews, who, in their turn, were to him an object of ridicule and contempt. Trusting in the power of the Roman army, by which he was supported, and in the favor of the Emperor, he laughed at the mutterings of the discontented people, as long as they did not disturb his comfort. Only when one or the other of those rebellious spirits, more daring or more ambitious than the rest, became too obnoxious to him, he nodded his head, and the noise-maker paid the penalty for his rashness by a slow death of starvation upon a cross or by the more merciful punishment of execution by the sword.

He was a great profligate; but his profligacy would not have been an object of serious reprobation by the Jews, who were themselves an indolent and profligate people, if he had not continually offended their vanity by treating them and their religion with mockery and disdain; but under the existing circumstances, his licentiousness formed one more welcome pretext for the discontented people to denounce him in private and to point at him scornfully and hatefully whenever it could be done without any risk to themselves.

He was married to an Arabian princess, the daughter of a neighboring king. His wife was a beautiful, modest, and unpretending woman; but having become satiated with her charms, he became subject to an animal passion for *Herodias*, the daughter of his half-brother. This proud and ambitious woman accepted his proposals, and to remove the most important impediment in the way for the accomplishment of his incestuous design, the king made up his mind to murder his wife. The plan failed, because the queen, having discovered the plot through the information received by a faithful servant, fled with a few trustworthy friends across the frontier to Arabia, to seek refuge in the house of her parents. This incident and the circumstances connected with it created a great scandal all over the country; but Herodes, infuriated at thus having the mask torn from his face, considered any further attempt at secrecy unnecessary, and resolved to defy public opinion. He therefore took Herodias to his court, and lived with her in open disregard of all decency and propriety.

Thus we often see that the great king of selfishness in Man is more enamoured of some Vice generated by the reasoning intellect, the half-brother of Wisdom, than of his legitimate wife, Knowledge, the daughter of Intuition; and when the latter sends her faithful servant, whose name is Conscience, to him, to reproach him for his infidelity, he attempts to kill her and drive her away from his heart. But when Conscience has once departed, Vice begins to show herself openly in defiance of all restraint.

Among those who most denounced his immorality was John the Baptist. Fearless and uncompromising, his voice thundered like the roar of a lion through the desert, and its echo was heard at the palace of the Tetrarch. Death and destruction and a day of judgment were foretold by the prophet, and repentance enjoined. Tyranny, vanity, and cowardice always go hand in hand; and for a while Herodes became seriously frightened. Thinking that at all events it might be well to make an attempt to escape the penalty due for his sins, he sent to John to inquire by what means the angry God could be pacified. John, however, was inexorable. He replied that divine justice could not be bribed or bargained with. No prayer, no sacrifice, no ceremony, he said, would avail. He demanded cessation of the incestuous intercourse, a return to Knowledge, and a separation from the ambitious woman.

Reproaches and accusations always smart when they are based upon truth. Such language Herodes was not accustomed to hear, nor would he submit to be made to appear to himself a villain. Still more angry was the beautiful Herodias, because she saw her plans for the future and her position threatened by the fanatical reformer. It required but little persuasion on her part to induce her lover to give the order for the arrest of John the Baptist, and to imprison him in the fortress of Makur.

More than this Herodes was not willing to do. He did not want to kill Reason, but he wanted to silence its voice whenever it was unwelcome to him. In vain Herodias wept and represented to him that John deserved to be punished by death, and that she could not be contented as long as the prophet was permitted to live, because his very presence was a reproach to her. Herodes knew that John, who was of a noble family, had many influential friends, and that to kill him would be to court an open rebellion; but there was still another cause which prevented him from consenting to the request of Herodias and to murder the prophet; for he suspected that perhaps, after all, the prophecies foretold by John might come true; and if so, what better means of protection against the ills that were to come, could he find than the prophet himself, who might act as his counsellor.

Moreover, John, imprisoned in the subterranean dungeons below the castle of Makur, was there as little capable of annoying the king, as if he had been already dead. There he might preach and denounce as much as he pleased; there was no one to listen to him. He therefore treated the requests of Herodias for the death-punishment of John the Baptist, as the results of a womanish whim, and he at last forbade her to mention this subject again.

But who can baffle the designs of a woman whose vanity has been offended? Who can silence the voice of vice, if reason is not permitted to speak? Herodias knew the weak points in the character of Herodes, — his sensuality and love of pleasure, his lewdness and pride, — and she resolved to have recourse to a trick, to extort from him that which she no longer dared to ask.

Herodias, as may well be imagined, was a beautiful woman. Stately was her form, and faultless her features. From her large dark eyes, overshadowed by long, drooping lashes, seemed to flash a supernatural fire, which made men her slaves, while a bewitching smile played around her lips, as if she were rejoicing over the victories she so easily gained over the senses of men. Her bearing was full of haughtiness and pride: thus must Judith have looked as she entered the tent of Holofernes to cut off the head of the king; thus may have looked Messalina when she feasted upon Roman patrician blood. But while she might have been regarded as an incarnation of pride, and a personification of lust, she appeared nevertheless very modest. These lips which seemed to scorn the world, could flatter and plead, this graceful form could bow down at the approach of the royal voluptuary, and submit to the embraces of one whom she despised at heart.

What did she care for Herodes? His person was nothing to her but an instrument by which she hoped to attain that which she desired,—the crown. If he had not been a king, she would have spurned him and detested his touch; but she well knew that the surest way for a woman to render a man her slave, is to appear to be submissive to him, and to obey his wishes even before they are uttered. Thus she ruled over Herodes, while Herodes dreamed of ruling over her.

She had committed a mistake by asking of him the life of John the Baptist; she ought to have been more careful, and induced Herodes to offer that life to her spontaneously, and apparently without her request. This mistake had to be remedied; for the head of John the Baptist had to fall, if she did not want to live in constant dread of his influence. "Who is this John," she said to herself, "that we should hesitate to put him to death? A beggar, like so many others that we have silenced when they became too noisy, and no one dared to reproach us for it. He, a worm, has dared to crawl into my path, and to oppose my will. I will not recede; I will crush him under my foot and go on: let his blood come upon himself."

She had asked for a clandestine interview with *Kaiphas*, the high-priest of the temple at Jerusalem, and one night he came to her in disguise. She asked him for his aid to annihilate John the Baptist, or to find a pretext to have the prophet accused and condemned by law as a heretic and infidel; but while Kaiphas offered no serious objection to the imprisonment of the prophet, whose violent speeches were liable to produce a schism in the church and to lessen the authority of the clergy, he would not listen to any proposals in regard to his murder; for John was of his caste, — even if he was a renegade, — and he harbored a certain amount of admiration for him.

Thus the beautiful Herodias was left to her own resources. She once attempted to have recourse to some practices of sorcery, in which she had received instruction from an Egyptian woman; but her ceremonies were of little avail, because the powers of evil which she invoked could not affect the pure soul of John the Baptist: they reverted to her own bosom and filled her heart with despair.

But if the powers of darkness were not able to do her bidding, there was a being, ever ready to comply with her wishes, namely, her own daughter *Salome*, the fruit of a former marriage of Herodias; a charming girl of about fifteen years, who was universally acknowledged to be the most beautiful young lady at the court of Herodes, and a most graceful dancer; and it had not escaped the attention of Herodias, that the eyes of the lascivious king often rested with a passionate glare upon the unripe charms of her daughter.

One day Salome had found her mother in tears, and after begging her to confess the cause of her sorrow, Herodias took her daughter into her confidence and confided her secret to her. Then the two women concocted a plan which was to cost John the Baptist his life. Salome was not a malicious girl; but she was exceedingly frivolous, inconsiderate, and vain, and flattered herself she was able to accomplish a thing in which even her mother had failed to succeed, and to outwit the king. As to John the Baptist, she cared no more for him than if he had been a slave.

In pursuance of the plot into which they had entered, Herodias made arrangements for a great festival to be held at Makur, to celebrate the birthday of the king. To that place the court resorted with a gathering of selected guests. Herodes was to be surprised by the magnificence of the feast.

The banquet was opened in a large hall of the castle. On three sides of the room tables and couches were arranged in horse-shoe form, opening towards the entrance, which was hung with heavy curtains. In the midst of the half-circle upon a somewhat elevated platform there was a throne for the king and Herodias, while at both sides the courtiers and the ladies were seated. Costly wines and rich viands were served, music and songs and various plays increased the hilarity of those present, but the best of all the performances was to come off at midnight.

At that time a number of selected beauties of Jerusalem, expert dancers, entered. They were dressed and ornamented in a manner calculated rather to expose their charms than to hide them. They performed an Arabian dance, that excited the senses of the half-drunken king to the utmost degree. But now in the midst of it the dancers made room, the heavy curtain opened, and Salome the beautiful whirled into the room, nude, excepting a transparent film-like texture, thin as a spider's web, serving as an ornament during her dance. As the beauty of the moon, the queen of the night, surpasses the stars, so the beauty of Salome outshone the rest of the dancers, as she went through the most graceful gyrations. Her magnetic gaze was directed upon the king, as if he were the sole object of her desires and the rest of the assembly did not exist for her; and when the dance ended and a storm of applause filled the room, she stood before the king, looking imploringly at him, her hands folded over her palpitating bosom. She was the personification of vanity and desire.

"A kingly entertainment, indeed!" stuttered the intoxicated Tetrarch, who had not recovered from his surprise.

"And worthy of a kingly reward!" said Herodias, in a loud voice, so that all present could hear it.

This remark excited the pride of Herodes. "Yes!" he said; "ask whatever thou desirest, and thou shalt receive it from me."

"Then give me at once the head of John the Baptist, laid upon a golden plate," answered Salome.

For a moment the king stared at her in terror and in surprise. He saw that he had been outwitted; but he was too proud to retract his promise, and, as if ashamed of his hesitation, he answered with a forced laugh and sent one of the most stalwart servants immediately to execute the command.

The above is an account of events supposed by many to have taken place in Palestine at the beginning of the Christian era, although there is no historical evidence for it; but what every one may know by his own self-examination is, that in the kingdom of the soul of semi-animal man selfishness is the king, represented as Herodes; and the voice of reason, represented as John the Baptist, cries like a voice in the wilderness. In many cases man does not wish to listen to that voice, nor does he wish to destroy it, unless, reduced by Passion, the daughter of Desire, he complies with her request, destroys his own reason, and thereby himself.

JERUSALEM.

The Truth is self-existent and independent of the opinions of men. It has not a stone upon which to rest its head, nor does it require any logical argument to support it. It is known to all who are willing to receive it when it enters their heart.

A CRY of indignation arose all over Judea when the foul murder of John the Baptist became known. The rich and the poor alike denounced, in unmeasured terms, that act of tyranny and cowardice. It seemed as if this had been the straw that broke the long-enduring camel's back, and in many parts of the country an open rebellion was threatened; for John was not merely a general favorite with the people and the accepted prophet of the Nazarenes; he was also of the Levitic caste, whose members were considered sacred. Now was the time for the long-expected Saviour to come. If he had appeared at that time and proved his authority by a few miracles, he would have had no end of admirers; but the redeemer did not come.

The Romans, full of security in their superior strength, remained quiet and looked upon the existing confusion as disinterested spectators. They knew that there was no hero among the Jews who could act as a leader, and the few persons who were inclined to act as such, counteracted each other's efforts by their own petty envies and jealousies. The Jews claimed that something must be done, but there was no one to do it; they all waited for Jehovah to perform some miracle, but the miracle was not performed; nor would an open rebellion without a great and heroic leader have been successful, for the Romans were well prepared for such an event; and although they seemed to be inactive, they silently took measures to suppress an insurrection. They acted wisely in not irritating the excited populace, for soon the sensation caused by the murder ceased to be a novelty; bread-and-butter affairs became again more important in their eyes than politics, and even the noisiest braggarts who had fought great battles with their tongues, quieted down.

At the beginning of the excitement Jehoshua was travelling in Judea; but when he heard of the murder of John the Baptist, he returned to his friends, the Nazarenes, to consult with them what measures were to be taken. He well knew that while the passions were raging, it would be useless for him to preach the gospel of wisdom to a people whose reason was dead, and any attempt on his part to occupy the position of a leader would have immediately caused him to be suspected of being a political agitator. To occupy such a position was not his desire. It was not his intention to interfere with the political institutions of the country; but to raise humanity up to a higher region of thought, to bring them nearer to a realization of the nature of true manhood, and to elevate their character and their sense of morality, upon which a change for the better in their external condition would follow as a natural consequence.

All external conditions are the outcome of internal conditions. This is as true in regard to a people as it is true in regard to a man, a society, an animal, a plant, or a rock. We cannot change the nature of a tree by trimming its branches; we cannot change the character of an animal by depriving it of its limbs; we cannot change the character and the natural conditions of a people by forcing upon it conditions which are unnatural, because they are not the outcome of interior growth. The law of *Karma* is an universal law which acts within communities, yea, even within solar systems, as it acts in regard to individuals. (A vice forcibly repressed, unless displaced by a virtue, will accumulate strength until the pent-up force is followed by an explosion.) Man is whatever he makes himself by his thoughts. A people on the whole may be looked upon as a compound individual, made up of a great many personalities, and yet being one entity to which the same law applies. A vicious man would drop back into vice to-morrow, if his sins were forgiven to-day; a people that cannot bear freedom would soon return to slavery, even if they were liberated by some miracle-worker.

Individuals, as well as communities, grow spiritually in proportion as they rise up to a higher ideal. If their ideal is lowered, they sink; if it becomes exalted, they will be elevated accordingly; slavery is an unnatural condition for men, but a natural condition for slaves; freedom is only made for the free. What will merely external reforms amount to, as long as the heart is not reformed? Does a villain become less of a villain if we dress him in beautiful garments? What will it serve to cut the branches of evil as long as the roots and the trunk remain? Heroes are the product of the growth of ideas. Reformers come when the time for reform is ripe; if they appear and bloom prematurely, they will produce no fruits. Luther and Napoleon were the products of their times; they did not create reforms before the necessity for reform had created them; the characters that appear upon the stage of life are the products of previously existing ideas; external life is merely a shadow-picture, representing upon the wall of matter the picture contained within the *magic lantern* of the mind. Ideas are everything; personalities, if compared with ideas, are nothing. Persons are only useful if they are instruments for the execution of ideas; a person who is not a vehicle for an idea is merely a corpse.

Long-continued and abject fear of Jehovah had made the Jews a nation of cowards. They had no power to help themselves, because they excluded the saving grace of God from their hearts. They needed an external saviour, an outward redeemer, one that would come riding upon the clouds, presenting credentials to secure an undisputed belief in his authority to save; a god, invested with thunder and lightning to destroy their oppressors. They were a people amongst whom individual selfishness had become so concentrated, that no true patriotism was to be found. There was at that time no *Marcus Curtius* among them, willing to sacrifice his personal self for the benefit of his country; those who were called patriots, were inspired by the love of self and of vanity; they expected to receive some reward from almighty Jehovah.

The more their self-confidence failed, the louder became their appeals to the god which they had created in their imagination. The odor arising from burning bodies of animals went uninterruptedly up to the clouds, to tickle the nostrils of the sleepy deity, to wake him up and induce him to fulfil his promises and to send the long-expected redeemer: but Jehovah would not awaken.

Such times were propitious to increase the authority of the priest and to fill the money-bags of the church. Not to allow any profit to escape the clutches of the church, the temples were partly turned into stables and bazaars, where animals of various kinds, such as were used for sacrifice, were kept for sale. Cattle and sheep, goats and pigeons, were waiting for the priestly butcher knife, to have their throats cut after a bargain was made. Helpless beasts were killed to please the bloodthirsty god; while those who killed them suffered ferocious monsters to grow up within their own souls.

Those who speculate upon human vanity and greed, easily accomplish their purpose. At those times the ignorant believed that to obtain gifts from God, it was necessary to make gifts to the church; then as now those who were able to pay for expensive ceremonies and church-service were considered the most pious and worthy to be respected. Well may the better-informed Pharisee then as now have laughed in his sleeve at the foolishness of the pilgrim who emptied his savings into the treasury of the church, to buy with material wealth things which could exist nowhere but in his own imagination; but deception was considered to be unavoidable and necessary, to secure a firm footing for the church in the hearts of the people and to keep them in subjection to the laws of order.

Clad in long-flowing robes, upon which were embroidered in gold, sentences from the sacred scrolls, the Pharisees went about public places, praying in loud voices and making a public display of their piety. No more did God speak in the hearts of men, for men had lost their power to hear; but instead of the voice of God they heard the voice of the priests, who claimed to be the keepers of the truth. They said that their words were the words of God, and to prove their authority pointed to the books of the law and the prophets and explained them in a manner most suitable to the interests of the church. But the people believed what they were told, for their John the Baptist was dead, having been killed by their own Herodes, and could not enlighten them in regard to this matter.

Owing to the ignorance and selfishness of the scribes,

external worship had become entirely divorced from the internal one, and empty forms and ceremonies were considered of far more importance than knowledge. Religion became a servant of clerical interests, and matters of theology became mixed up with political affairs.

(All attempts to unite the interests of church and state will always degrade religion and weaken the state by creating a rival power within the latter. True Religion has no other interest but the ennobling of the soul; she is above all temporal and egoistic considerations; she does nothing for the purpose of gaining material wealth or to gratify personal ambition; such things are done by the church, but not by religion.) A government that needs the assistance of priestcraft to frighten the people into submission is a government of slaves, and itself a slave to the church. It is weak, and becomes still weaker by dividing its power with the Pharisees. Religion ought never to be used as a means to accomplish an unreligious purpose; true religion has for its purpose the final union of Man with the universal God, and rests upon a knowledge of the nature of the relations existing between God and Man; but the foundation upon which priestcraft rests is the self-love of man and his desire to obtain rewards which he does not deserve. This selfishness is inherent in the animal nature of Man; it is the rock upon which sectarianism rests, and it is as everlasting as the mountains; for as long as men exist in semi-animal forms, their higher aspirations will be mixed with selfish desires. As long as they possess no knowledge of self, they will be helpless and ignorant; as long as they cannot protect themselves against their own selves, they will look to the state for the protection of their bodies, and to the church for the salvation of their souls. They may do away with certain forms of superstition and abolish some creed; they may for a time imagine themselves to be free; but as long as they are not free from their own selfish desires, they cannot be really free: for the devil who keeps them in chains is within their own selves; he goes with them to the church and wherever they go. If they do away with one superstition, it will be merely to replace it by another; if they break the chains of one master, they will soon crave for another to protect them against their own selves.

As long as men are not able to govern their own desires, as long as they possess merely opinions but not knowledge, they cannot be free, and require a master to lead them; but they have a right to demand that their master should know more than they know themselves, and that he should assist them in gaining knowledge and not force them to remain ignorant. However much it may be in the interest of mankind to attain knowledge, it is not in the interests of their masters that they should attain it; for if men were to attain knowledge, they would become free and need no other master but their own selves. Thus the interests of priestcraft are in continual conflict with religion, and will remain so until mankind comes a step nearer to God in spite of the resistance offered by the church.

Woe to the church that speculates upon the ignorance of mankind; it will be a power of evil and perish in darkness. Woe to the state that cannot stand without being propped up by the church. It may find the support pleasant and useful, but the time may come when the spirits that have been evoked grow strong and will not retire at our bidding, and they then become a curse to the country and overpower the state that called them to its aid.

At the time of which we are writing, the alliance between the state and the church at Jerusalem was not very strong; for the views of the Romans in regard to theology were different from those of the Jews. But the Roman government recognized the rights of the *Sanhedrin* to have laws of its own, and it even lent its aid to enforce these laws; and thus while the want of energy among the Jews, originating in their religious beliefs, made it easy for the Romans to keep the Jews in subjection, the recognition of the temporal authority of the church created—so to say—a Jewish government within the Roman government, weakening the latter and producing conflicts between the two, besides nourishing a rebellious spirit among the Jews, which had to be kept down by the overwhelming power of the Romans.

Similar conditions may be found to exist even at this day in that "Jerusalem" known as the Mind of Man. In a well-governed Mind the king of Reason enlightened by Wisdom ought to rule supreme; but if he forms an alliance with Selfishness, Reason will lose its power, and a kingdom of Ignorance will be established within the kingdom of Reason. Then will the edicts of the "church" enter in conflict with the laws given by the legitimate ruler, and Reason will be lost unless Wisdom comes to its aid.

Thus the processes that are continually going on within the Mind of individual men resemble the processes taking place within the Mind of Humanity; and as the thoughts of individual man find outward expression in his features and in his acts, likewise the thoughts of Humanity find expression in personalities and historical events; for the visible world is nothing else but a stage upon which the inner life of humanity is enacted, a place where man's subjective and real existence finds an external representation in that sphere of illusions called the physical world.

THE GREAT RENUNCIATION.

> We can attain the High only by rising above that which is low. The life of the God in Man necessitates the sacrifice of his attraction to the animal elements existing in his constitution.

GREAT was the joy with which the Nazarenes welcomed him whom they now recognized as their Master. His mind had expanded, his spirituality had become strong, and his very presence seemed awe-inspiring and holy. There was no wavering or uncertainty in his decisions; he had grown to that full stature in which man's thoughts become his words, and words become acts; he had gained the power to control his own mind, and in doing so he controlled the minds of others. His superiority was so self-evident, that his former friends now became his disciples, and his followers looked upon him as if he were something more than mortal, — a god. Nor was such a belief unjustifiable; for he had become so much united to his own divine inner Self, that the divinity of the latter seemed to permeate even his mortal frame and to attract to itself other spiritual influences of the same kind, whose presence was manifested on several occasions.

Thus once he went with some of his disciples upon the top of a high mountain, and as he stood there, he became deeply immersed in meditation, while his companions, not wishing to disturb the sacred silence, watched him from the distance. Then it appeared to them as if a light of a supernatural kind were emanating from him, and in that light they beheld the presence of two Adepts, whom they supposed to be Moses and Elias of old.

Such an occurrence need not be regarded as impossible or incredible by the sceptic. The Higher Self, the divine *Adonai*, the "Spirit" of Man, is not a poetical fancy or a metaphysical hypothesis to those who have risen up to his sphere. There are perhaps few persons who have not at least once in their lives, perhaps during the days of their childhood, felt that such a "guardian spirit" was near, and there is abundant evidence in the biographies of heroes and saints, in ancient and modern history, going to show that man's Higher Self may manifest itself visibly to the lower self, and that it may have spiritual intercourse with its own equals, in the same sense as a mortal man may communicate with other mortals upon this earth.

As to the nature of man's divine Self we are informed by the ancient Bhagavad Gita, that: "In this world there are two existences, the perishable and the imperishable. The Perishable consists of all living things, (the Senses, etc.); the Imperishable is called the *Lord on high*. But there is another, the highest existence, called the *Supreme Spirit*, who as the eternal Lord (Iswara)[1] pervades the three worlds and sustains them";

[1] The *Logos* (Christ), John x. 9.

and we are furthermore informed by the same source, that: "Some by meditation perceive the soul within themselves by themselves . . . , while others, who know it not, hear of it from others, and worship, and these too, devoted to the sacred doctrine, pass over death."

These views are amply corroborated by the teachings of Jehoshua, who speaks of himself on many occasions, as if he had become one with that divine Self, while the apostle Paul and others repeat the same doctrine in regard to the corruptible and incorruptible body.[1]

Again he began to teach in the towns of Galilee and Judea, and more than ever his fame spread over the country and penetrated even within the walls of Jerusalem. The members of his family, who were astonished to see him acquire such a renown, went to him, to claim him as one of their own. But Jehoshua had outgrown that stage in which ties of blood form any attraction to man; he had become one with his soul, and that soul was not the son of a mortal woman. He was a genius, and the Universal Spirit his Father; he was above all terrestrial considerations, living entirely in the realm of the Ideal. Our parents are the progenitors of the physical forms which man temporarily inhabits during his earthly life; but that form is not the real self of the regenerated man, who existed from all eternity.[2]

Jehoshua therefore said: "Who is my mother, and who are my brethren? He who does the will of our

---

[1] Colossians i. 27. II. Corinthians iv. 16. I. Corinthians xv. 53.
[2] John v. 26.

eternal Father is my brother, my sister, and mother." [1] He was so taken up and absorbed by the one grand idea of universal fraternal Love, that he lost sight of the earthly ties that bind personalities to each other. In his superior state he ceased to be an individual man in all but external form; it was as if his soul had become unconscious of inhabiting a separate state of existence, and had mixed with the universal indivisible divine Spirit.

How can such a superior state be realized by those who cling to the illusion of Self? How can it be understood by an age whose fundamental principle upon which its religion and science, politics and social intercourse are based, is the illusion of Self, and to which a renunciation of personal existence appears to be identical with annihilation? And yet Christians claim to believe such things in theory; for the fundamental doctrine upon which original Christianity was founded is the sacrifice of personal existence, which leads to a resurrection in a life beyond personality and mortality.

What is the signification of the Christian *Cross?* Is it merely a memento of an historical event, to remind the present generation that some eighteen hundred years ago, an honest man was executed as a criminal by being nailed to a cross? Then if that man or God had been executed by means of a gallows, a gallows would have become the emblem of the Christian faith, and

[1] Matthew xii. 50.

gallows in the place of crosses would now be seen in churches and houses and upon the tops of the spires of Christian places of worship. No! The *Cross* has a far deeper signification; it is a symbol that was known thousands of years before the advent of modern Christianity; it may be found in Indian cave-temples and upon relics dating from antediluvian times. It cannot mean the death of a god, for gods are immortal and cannot be killed; it means the entire cessation of all thoughts of self — of all self-love, self-will; it means the *mystic death*, the renunciation of everything belonging to personality and limitation, and the entering in a life in the Infinite, Unlimited, and Eternal. This renunciation of Self is the great "stone of contention" in the way of those who desire to become immortal while they yet cling to their personal self.[1] This superior state is one of spiritual consciousness above all sense of personality; it is a happy, and therefore a "heavenly," state. It requires no keys of bishop or pope, nor any permission to be obtained by a clergyman, to enter its portals; it merely requires the power and the ability to give up one's love for the lower self and to join the consciousness of the Higher Self, which already exists in "heaven."

How could the prohibition of a priest or the malediction of a pope ever prevent a man from rising up to a higher region of thought or entering a higher state of consciousness? If man's soul is able to wing itself up to

[1] Matthew viii. 35.

those celestial heights, no interdict will be able to prevent it. How could the permission of a church enable man to enter into a region of thought which he is not able to enter, because he clings with the grasp of despair to his lower perishing self? Verily a church claiming such a power is like the Pharisees of old, of whom Jehoshua said: "Woe to you, hypocrites! who devour the widows' houses, pretending to give spiritual gifts, while you do not possess them yourselves." [1]

This doctrine of the entire renunciation of Self is the great mystery which the Spirit of Christ has taught at all times through the mouths of the sages; it is the great secret which Jehoshua vainly attempted to bring to the understanding of a selfish nation; it is the great truth which Divine Wisdom still continues to teach. Jehoshua's disciples did not grasp this idea; for when he explained to them that it was necessary to give up personal existence, to gain that life which is eternal, "they refused to go any further with him." They, too, dreamed of a sensual heaven; their aspirations did not rise higher than to gain an everlasting terrestrial life in a material heaven, where, unburdened from gross matter, their astral *egos* might enjoy a life resembling the one upon this planet, but without the sufferings of the latter; a life where there are still personal likes and dislikes, attractions and desires, social intercourse and amusements; a life in a limited, although ethereal form, full of change, and therefore not self-existent and not eternal.

[1] Matthew xxiii. 14.

But Jehoshua spoke of a heavenly state, where no one is married nor given in marriage; where there is no distinction of sex or race or of religious opinion; where each individual soul is a spiritual power, a note in the great symphony that constitutes the harmony of the All; a state in which we will all be *one in Divinity*, as we are now *one in Humanity;* an existence where all are cemented together by the universal principle of Love, where individual consciousness is swallowed up in the inconceivable happiness of eternal and universal existence, of which men cannot conceive intellectually as long as they cling to form, and which is therefore like nothing to them.

A kingdom after this pattern Jehoshua wanted to establish even on this earth. He wanted to unite all mankind by the power of fraternal love, to do away with injustice, superstition, and priestcraft, to bring each individual up to a conscious realization of his own divine nature, to induce men to cultivate their spiritual talents and to develop the spiritual powers which slumber in every soul. He well knew that all men are not alike, and that there can be no external equality upon the material plane as long as the process of evolution lasts. Permanent equality would mean a permanent cessation of progress; it would be characterized by an absence of that necessary stimulus which causes activity; but he knew that all men had the same natural rights for the attainment of knowledge, and that they all were entitled to see the truth and to strive after supreme and eternal happiness. He wanted to give them a higher, a *true* Ideal, which would raise them up into the highest regions of thought to a nobler conception of Man, and thus by ennobling them save them even from their material degradation, by and through their own efforts.

Great is the power of Wisdom! It captivates even those who are not able to see it, provided they do not wilfully repel its light when it seeks to enter the heart. The soul feels the power of wisdom, even if the intellect cannot grasp it. The doctrines of Jehoshua captivated the minds of the people; they began to look upon him as the promised saviour, who had come to destroy their enemies, to make the poor equals of the rich, and to supply all with comfort and happiness. Some believed him to be an incarnation of John the Baptist; others imagined they beheld in him the spiritual power of an *Avatar*. The Pharisees and the scribes of the temple at Jerusalem searched their sacred scrolls; but they could find no prophecy of any star that was to arise from Nazareth; they would not believe that any good could come out of that place. His language sounded insulting to them, because it exposed their failings; his doctrines were undermining the foundation upon which their church and its dogmas rested. He deserved death, and it was necessary by all means to secure his person, to prevent further mischief to the interests of the church. In Galilee he was secure as long as he created no political trouble with the Romans; the authority of the temple of Jerusalem did not extend beyond certain limits. They consulted with each other about means to coax him to come to Jerusalem; they tried to bribe his family to induce him to go there, and his brothers advised him to go.[1]

The idea of going to Jerusalem, to give the finishing stroke to his work, had already entered the mind of Jehoshua. He well knew the dangers connected with such an attempt; but now he had grown strong and powerful and risen above all personal considerations. His personal safety seemed to him not worthy of a moment's thought; it was the truth — not his person — that he desired to defend; and if his mortal body were to die in his attempt at defending the truth, the cause which he advocated could only gain by such a sacrifice.

In vain his friends pleaded that he should not thus risk his life. Dark clouds of the future rose up before his clairvoyant vision; but above these clouds he saw a light, as if a thousand suns were bursting forth in the sky, filling infinite space with its glory. He beheld his human personality like a hardly perceptible speck of dust in the boundless ocean of matter. Was it worth while to consider what became of such an insignificant thing, when the whole of humanity was to be saved from ignorance?

Let the would-be wise of the world call such a state of mind a product of a "morbid imagination," "hallucination," or whatever they please. To the vulgar every-

[1] John vii. 3.

thing is vulgar, and the worm crawling under the ground can realize nothing else but the presence of earth. To the coward, courage would be an abnormal state; to the stingy, generosity is a pathological condition; to the foolish, knowledge belongs to the unknowable; to the selfish, unselfishness is an absurdity. When our philosophers will be able to answer intelligently the question, What is *Matter?* then will it be time for them to study what is *Consciousness* or *Spirit.* When our anthropologists will have learned something more about the constitution of Man than merely his phenomenal aspect, when our naturalists will know more than the mere superficial laws of nature, and our "Divines" are divine in truth and not merely in name, then will it be time to argue the questions of eternity and immortality with them. Until that time arrives, "the wisdom of the worldly wise will be foolishness in the eyes of Divine Wisdom."[1]

In our utilitarian age the most useless things are looked upon as Real and Useful, and that which is of the highest use in the end is regarded as an Illusion. Matter is said to be all, and Spirit is said to be nothing. But of what use would Matter be without life and without thought? how could we utilize Matter, if we had no Intellect to employ it, and what is the Intellect but an activity of matter produced by the stimulus coming from what is called "Spirit" or *God?*

The time of the festival of the *Tabernacles* was ap-

[1] John vii. 3.

proaching, and this was considered by Jehoshua as the most appropriate time for his visit to the capital of Judea. At that time the city would be filled with great crowds from the country, upon whose good natural common sense he might rely to a certain extent, because they were less sophisticated than the inhabitants of the city, whose opinions and sentiments change like the wind, where a hero may be glorified to-day and stoned to death to-morrow.

The followers of Jehoshua saw that the storm was approaching. Some of the more timid ones began to regard him as a fanatic, whose rashness was about to bring on his destruction, and they silently retired to their homes. Others believed that the long-expected day of judgment was about to appear and that some great miracle was to take place. They went with him, because they hoped to get some celestial reward, and they already began to dispute which one of them would be the greatest in heaven. Many believed that he would never reach Jerusalem alive, that the priests would cause him to be murdered on the way, to avoid the sensation which was certain to be created by his open arrest. Perhaps on account of these considerations Jehoshua kept his plan secret and did not start for the capital with the usual caravan, but left soon afterwards by a different route, going by the way of *Sichem* and through the country of the *Samaritans*, known as the place where works of charity are performed.

It is said that when he entered Jerusalem, he rode

upon an ass: nor could it have been otherwise; for the truth cannot enter the soul of man unless sitting upon the ass of self-conceit, and those who attempt to enter the temple of knowledge carrying that ass on their backs will be left outside.

THE TEMPLE.

There is only one Temple in which the Truth can manifest its divinity; it is that living and conscious organism which constitutes the soul and body of Man.

THE unexpected arrival of Jehoshua at Jerusalem was to the Pharisees of the temple like a thunderbolt coming from a clear sky. They had given up all hopes of drawing him into their net, and believed that he would not dare to come to Jerusalem, and now the bird arrived voluntarily and without any coaxing. But the bird was an eagle, and was likely to tear the meshes with his claws and punish his assailants with his beak.

The first information they received of the arrival of their enemy came through the triumphal shouts of the multitude at the temple, to which Jehoshua had immediately gone and where he inspired his hearers with the living fire of truth that came from his heart.

They went to the place where he spoke and they asked him by what authority he was teaching, and he answered them that he taught by the authority of that omnipotent power which inspired the ancient prophets; but that only those who were true themselves would be able to perceive the truth speaking in him; and when they asked him to prove that his doctrines were true, he said: "The doctrines which I teach are not my own, but it is the Truth which teaches them through me. He that teaches his own doctrines and theories speaketh of himself; he is acting under the impulse of earthly ambition and seeketh his own glory and not the glory of God; but he that seeks to glorify, — not himself, — but God, by giving expression to the truth of which he is conscious, is true, and no evil can be in him.[1] Live so, that you may know the truth, not by external appearances and argumentation, but by its own inherent power.[2] Be true, and you will know the truth."[3]

"The organism of Man," he said, "resembles a kingdom; its capital is the Mind, and its temple the soul. In that capital and temple there are many false prophets, as there are in Jerusalem. There are the Pharisees of sophistry and false logic, credulity, and scepticism; and the 'scribes' are the prejudices and erroneous opinions engrafted upon the memory. Do not listen to what these false prophets say, but listen to the voice of wisdom that speaks in your heart; for verily I say unto you, the temple, built of speculations which the scribes have erected, will be destroyed, and not one of the dogmas and theories of which it has been constructed will remain, when the day of sound judgment appears.[4]

"See the truth enters your heart, bearing the palm leaf, the symbol of peace. Let it abide in you, and abide yourself in the truth. There is no other worship

---

[1] John vii. 16.
[2] John vii. 24.
[3] John viii. 47.
[4] Matthew xxiv. 2.

acceptable to the universal God, but to keep his commandments, which he reveals to you through the power of Divine Wisdom, whose voice speaks in your higher consciousness. Love one another; and as you grow in unselfish love, so will you grow in wisdom.

"Those who are seeking for Truth in external things will not find it, for the external world is merely a world of appearances, and not of absolute truth. The Spirit of God is pervading the universe, but the physical senses are not constituted to see it; neither can the finite intellect comprehend the Infinite. Seek for divine wisdom within yourself; then will God come to reside in you, and you will find him. He that hates the truth hates God, for the Truth is divine and comes from God. If you let the spirit of Wisdom abide in your hearts, it will guide you into the light of knowledge; but when it departs from your heart, then will you abide in the darkness of ignorance, and your soul will weep and lament, but the animal instincts within you will rejoice, for they love darkness and are sorely grieved by the light of the truth.

"Open your hearts and see the image of the true God within them. He is not to be found in man-made temples and churches; and if any one tells you, Christ is in this church, or he is in that one, do not believe it, but seek for God within your own heart. Let not the Pharisees and the scribes and the intellectual powers of your mind mislead you, but listen to the divine voice of Intuition, which speaks at the centre of your own soul."

It may easily be imagined that such language exasperated the Pharisees and the sceptics; nor would it be tolerated by them to-day. They attempted to have Jehoshua arrested upon the spot, but they did not succeed, because the populace took his part. There is an eternal battle going on in the mind of man and on the external plane between error and truth, between speculation and intuition, between true religion and priestcraft, and the two combatants are often so intermingled with each other, that it is exceedingly difficult to distinguish them from each other and to tell where the truth ends and where falsehood begins. Every attack made upon the erroneous opinions and the selfishness of the church autocrats is misrepresented by the latter as an attack upon religion; not upon *their* religious views, but as an attack upon religion itself. Their church is their God, and the interests of the church are their religion; it is all the God and the religion they know; they can form no conception of a God without priestcraft, nor of a religion without church-benefits. Having all their lives kept their minds within the narrow grooves prescribed for them by their creeds, having become accustomed to worship an unnatural, limited, impossible, and helpless God, who needs the assistance of the clergy to teach mankind; the universal, omnipotent, omnipresent Divinity, *the Christ*, whose light shines into the hearts of men is non-existent to them; and although they preach such Christ with their mouths, repeating the sayings of the ancient books of wisdom, without understanding their meaning, nevertheless they deny him in practice and reject him on every occasion. They preach love and act hate; they claim to love God, but the God they love is fashioned after their own fancies, and by loving him, they love nothing else but themselves. Their God is a limited, personal, circumscribed and narrow-minded God, and their love is equally narrow-minded and intolerant.

Such and similar truths Jehoshua attempted to bring to the understanding of the people in the temple of Jerusalem. "The spirit of Wisdom," he said, "that speaks in me and through my lips, and whose voice every one of you might hear within his heart, if he knew how to listen to it, is the way, the truth, and the life. It is the light of the world, and he that followeth it, shall not walk in darkness, but shall have the light of life.[1] He who has become conscious of the existence of that light within his soul will not die, for he then lives in the light and the light lives in him.[2] I am not asking you to believe what Jehoshua says, but I ask you to seek for the truth within your own selves, so that you may *know* that the truth is speaking through me;[3] for the truth is self-evident to those that are true, and requires no other certificate but its own self.[4] I am not here to do the will of the terrestrial elements composing that frame, but to do the will of the Supreme Intelligence, from whom all spirits are born.[5] You are now

[1] John viii. 12. [2] John vi. 57. [3] John v. 30.
[4] John v. 36. [5] John vi. 38.

worshipping something of which you know nothing; but the time will come when men will rise up to an understanding of that God who is not a product of the imagination of man, and must be worshipped in spirit and in truth.[1] Salvation must come from within yourself; it does not come from without. It cannot be bought with sacrifices nor be conferred upon you by a clergyman, but it is attained by the sacrifice of yourself. If the spirit of God does not live within you, how can you expect to live?[2] for the spirit of God is Life and is immortal in Man. The gods which men have created are the servants of their churches; but the true God is greater than the church. There is no temple worthy to be the residence of the God of Humanity, but the living souls of those who are pure in their hearts.[3] There is no salvation without sanctification."[4]

Such unorthodox language was as intolerable to the Pharisees as it would be to their modern successors, if it were publicly repeated to-day. Such language, if tolerated, would overthrow the authority of the church and of that god who is believed to belong to the church. What would be the use for men to hire a priest to intercede with God, if God accepted no intercession? What would become of the doctrine which taught that the Jews were the favorite people of Jehovah, if Jehovah had no favorites and was no respecter of persons, but a universal Spirit, dispensing life and light to all

---

[1] John iv. 22.
[2] Romans viii. 8.
[3] Luke xvii. 21.
[4] Hebrews xii. 14.

without partiality? "This man," they said, "must surely be possessed of a devil"; and they consulted with each other how they might kill him; but they dared not to attack him openly, because he was very popular, for there were many among the crowd who had been mentally blind all their life, and who now became able to open their eyes and to see the light of the truth.

The people always admire courage and intrepidity; they well knew the dangers by which Jehoshua was surrounded, and the fact that he remained within the walls of Jerusalem and continued to teach in the temple, in spite of the threatening danger, gained for him their hearts.

There was an old law, which said that whoever attempted to create contempt for the prevailing methods of worship, or to cause disrespect in regard to the established forms of religion, should be stoned to death without the privilege of a hearing, without judgment, and without defence. According to this law, Jehoshua had many times incurred the penalty of death, but the Pharisees did not dare to arrest him, on account of his great popularity.

But an event occurred which brought on the end.

As the mind of man, the temple of the living God, becomes converted into a stable and trading shop, if selfishness is permitted to enter; likewise the temple of Jerusalem had become converted into a stable and market-hall by the selfishness of the Pharisees. The courts of the temple and even the interior halls were filled with stalls, where merchants sold their goods, and the noise made by the seller who praised his goods, and the buyer who attempted to cheapen the price, penetrated into the innermost sanctuary.

Grieved at this desecration, and while carried away by his ardor, he overthrew one of the stalls where trinkets were sold, and his enthusiastic listeners followed his example. Immediately the selfish passions of the audience were aroused; their instincts told them that an opportunity had arrived for plunder, and a fight ensued, during which the merchants lost their goods and were driven from the temple, while thieves enriched themselves with their stores.

This unfortunate occurrence broke the spell by which Jehoshua ruled the hearts of the people. | Brute force can never be an ally for the promulgation of the truth.) Wisdom is a spiritual power, and external measures are useless for its purpose unless they are guided by wisdom. For one moment only the great reformer had lost the mastery over himself, and now a crime had been committed. At that moment he had ceased to be a representative of the truth and become an offender — not merely against the laws of the church, but against the divine law of justice. As long as he contented himself with denouncing the selfishness of the Pharisees, he merely appealed to the power of reason, but by his perhaps involuntary and unpremeditated act, he had appealed to the unreasoning instincts of the populace and entered into relation with the elements of evil.

By this act he had ceased to be a reformer, and become a disturber of the peace.

The Pharisees were not slow to recognize the advantage they had gained by this event. They now appealed to the sense of justice and reason, and Jehoshua had to leave the city to avoid arrest. He went to the village of *Ephraim* and remained there with his disciples.

History is said to be always repeating itself. Even the Pharisees of the world and the reasoning powers in Man are willing to listen to the voice of the truth as long as it does not come in conflict with their selfish interests. All men admire the truth, as long as he remains in his cage and does not threaten their self-interest; but when he overthrows a favorite creed, then will they drive him away from the city. Then will the spirit of Wisdom have to retire to some quiet place, to wait until the storm of the passion has ceased, when it may again attempt to enter the heart.

THE HERO.

That which is impermanent and illusive depends for its existence on external conditions. That which is real and permanent finds the necessary conditions within itself.

It is not often that an error committed does not cause another. Jehoshua, in overthrowing the stall at the temple, had committed a mistake; his flight from Jerusalem was another one; it was dictated by prudence and necessary to save his person from danger, but personal considerations of any kind should never be allowed to enter the mind of the true Adept, if they are in conflict with justice. He who has risen entirely above the sphere of selfishness, to that plane to which few are able to rise, acts only in accordance with justice, — a justice blind to all personal claims. Such justice demanded that he should have remained and faced the consequences of the act for which he was morally responsible. He well knew that if he were to deliver himself to his enemies, it was not justice but revenge that would await him; but he perceived that it was wrong for him to have left Jerusalem, and that it would have been his duty to remain at his post. Moreover, the row at the temple had caused a misunderstanding in regard to the doctrines he taught, and it was necessary to correct this mistake.

His first act of imprudence could not be remedied — the stolen goods would not be restored; but to remedy the second mistake was in his power, and the fact that it was his duty to return to Jerusalem was strongly impressed upon his mind. In spite of the entreaties of his friends, he therefore resolved to return, and he selected for that purpose the approaching festival of the *Passover*.

From a worldly and personal point of view such a resolution appears absurd; but from the standpoint of the higher self it was reasonable, because it was right. His reason and logic told him that, while he would expose himself to a great danger if he returned to Jerusalem, he would probably not even find an opportunity to explain his position; but his intuition told him that by returning he would act in accordance with justice. The intellect argues and speculates to find out what may be true, but Wisdom knows the truth without any argumentation. His intellect told him not to expose his person to danger; but intuition told him to go without fear: for even if the Pharisees would take undue advantage of him and act unjustly towards his person, that was their own affair, which he had not to consider; for no man can be made responsible for any other acts than those which he performs himself or wilfully causes others to perform. Logic came and told him that it would be far more reasonable for him to escape, for he would be able to do a great deal more good for humanity by continuing to live, than if he were to go to the capital and permit himself to be killed by his enemies; but Divine Wisdom bade him to go to Jerusalem, and to leave the consequences to God.

The preparations for the Passover festival had begun; the city became filled with strangers, and once more Jehoshua and his disciples were on their way to Jerusalem. It was publicly known that the Sanhedrin had issued an order to have him arrested as soon as he should enter the gates of the city; and when it became known at Jerusalem, that in spite of the threatening danger he was on his way to return, his friends rejoiced at his courage, and they went to the suburb to meet him. They received him with exclamations of joy and made him ride in their midst. Thus they entered the gates and baffled the vigilance of the priests, who did not dare to arrest him while he was surrounded by so many adherents.

Thus does the soul of man rejoice when, after a period of darkness during which the truth had departed, and sin and selfishness assumed the rule, wisdom, the king and saviour, appears again at the gates. At such a solemn moment the passions flee to their dens, superstitions retire to their corners. Peace accompanies the king and enters with him, and the whole interior world is filled with light and resounds with solemn harmonies, while from all the *intelligent* powers arises a glad Hosanna.

But the priests and Pharisees well knew that their doom was approaching, unless they acted without further delay. If they permitted him to remain at Jerusalem, he would indeed become a king of the Jews; for he gained all hearts, not so much by his arguments as by that power by which a superior spirit obtains the mastery over the masses.

The arguments which Jehoshua used while teaching in the temple were indeed unanswerable and his doctrines were sublime; but his ideas were too grand to be understood by the people; they could not grasp them intellectually, but they intuitively knew that he was right, and they believed not merely in his words, but in *Him*.

The Pharisees consulted with each other, and they agreed that it was not advisable to attempt to arrest him during that day; they resolved to wait until the following night, and they bribed one of his followers to inform them about the place where Jehoshua was going to spend the night, so that they might secure his person without difficulty.

Thus, if the truth has once entered the soul and the inhabitants of the mind have become conscious of his presence, all selfish desires will become subject to his supreme rule; nor will it be possible for doubts to obtain mastery over the truth as long as the light of knowledge exists; but when the night of ignorance again appears, and the intelligent spiritual powers which accompany the king fall asleep, then will doubts again appear, and by bribing Logic, one of the disciples of Wisdom, they will induce him to use his sophistry and to traduce his Master; for this "*Judas Ischarioth*" is easily influenced by selfish desires and external illusions; it can easily be made to traduce and pervert the truth : but if it allows itself to be thus employed, it would be better it had never been born; for when the day of sound judgment appears and wisdom returns, then will this false logic be forced to destroy itself by its own power, and by its own deductions annihilate itself.

The nearer this fallacious logic approaches the truth, the more dangerous will it become; for an argument which is false and touches the truth, becomes a traitor to it. Only when Logic embraces the Truth and remains one with it, can it be trusted.

The chief priests and the elders of the temple arrived; and as they dared not capture him in the midst of the crowd, they attempted to mislead him with their arguments. They tempted him, and asked whether or not it was just that they should pay taxes to the *Emperor*, or whether they should give up their whole life to the contemplation of the things of the Spirit. And Jehoshua answered them in parables, teaching that as long as man is inhabiting a corporeal form, it is his duty to provide for that form; but that he should not give to Matter that which belongs to the Spirit. He said that while the labor of the body and intellect may be employed for terrestrial purposes, they themselves, being of a terrestrial nature, man's higher intelligent powers and aspirations should always be directed towards the Eternal. The body and Intellect of Man is his servant, and it is the duty of the Master to provide for the needs of the latter; but the Master must not become the slave of his servant by making his wisdom subservient to the intellect or by employing his reason for the gratification of the animal self.

Then spake Jehoshua to the multitude and to his disciples, and said: "The Scribes and the Pharisees (the intellectual reasoning powers of man) have occupied the chair belonging to Divine Wisdom. If men speak wisely, observe what they say; but very often they speak wise words and do not act wisely. The priests put heavy burdens upon the people, grievous to be borne, but they themselves will not — nor can they — lift a finger to move them. All the works they do, are done for the purpose of being seen and admired by men; they ornament their clothing and make big arguments, and broad borders to their garments. They love the uppermost rooms at the feast, and the chief seats in the synagogues; they want to be greeted in the markets and be called Rabbi, Rabbi; but be not ye called Rabbi, for one is your Master, *the Truth*, and all ye are brethren. Call no man your (spiritual) father (by adopting his opinion); for one is your *Father*, the consciousness of the Truth. The Intellect seems now to you to be the greatest of the powers of man; but it can only be the greatest, if it is illuminated by Wisdom.

"Woe to you, Scribes and Pharisees, for ye shut up the kingdom of heaven against men, by preventing them from attaining spiritual knowledge. Ye neither go in yourselves, neither will ye suffer them that are entering to go in. You send your missionaries to encompass sea and land to make one proselyte; and when he is made, ye make him twofold more the child of evil than yourself, because you teach him to argue and use sophistry, and to cling to external illusions. Woe unto you, who are blind to the spiritual perception of the truth, while you pretend to be the keepers of it, ye blind guides who strain at a gnat and swallow a camel. You are like whited sepulchres, which appear beautiful outward, but which are within full of dead men's bones and corruption. Wisdom has departed from you, and will not return until you give up your hypocrisy and selfishness, and learn to worship the truth.

"He who is filled with the spirit of wisdom, possessing spiritual knowledge, is the heaven-ordained priest, the true shepherd, and those who love the truth know his voice; but the merely man-ordained and selfish priests, full of vanity and having no truth in their hearts, are like thieves that enter the sheepfold, not through the legitimate door of direct perception, but by climbing in through the window of argumentation."

Such language was sufficient to wound the vanity of the Pharisees and their followers, and it was the more painful because it was true. Accusations or vilifications which are not just cause no pain to the self-conscious spirit; they drop like blunt arrows from the armor of him who rises above them; but the more an accusation approaches the truth, the more will it penetrate to the heart and cause a painful wound. If the death of Jehoshua had not been already resolved upon by the priesthood, this public exposition of their hypocrisy and untrustworthiness would have been sufficient to draw their venomous hate upon him : moreover, his death was now a matter of political necessity, for as long as the truth is permitted to remain, there is no security for priestcraft, sectarianism and erroneous opinions.

He had aroused the spirit of inquiry among the intelligent powers; he had dared to tear the masks from conceit and hypocrisy, and to hold up the nakedness of time-honored superstitions to public contempt, and he was hated and feared by the orthodox Jews. They desired to kill him, because Logic easily becomes the enemy of the truth if Selfishness whispers in his ear.

As a matter of course, it was not to be supposed that the crowds which listened to his language understood his ideas; for ideas, like trees, do not grow up and unfold in one day like a product of Magic; they require time to take root in the mind, to bring forth branches and leaves, to bear flowers and fruits; but some seeds had been laid in the soil, and some persons commenced to think; some of the intuitional powers within the mind had begun to wake up and become receptive. Some remained in that condition, while others went to sleep again, like a drunken man who opens his eyes as the thunder rolls in the sky, and then falls back again into his stupor.

It may be asked: "Why should mankind be disturbed in their happy dreams? Why should they be enlightened in regard to things which they do not care to know, being happy in their ignorance? Is not the object of life the attainment of happiness, and how could we convey a greater happiness upon mankind, than by saving them the trouble of thinking, by taking the labor for their salvation upon our shoulders, so that they may spend all their time for pleasure and for the acquisition of luxury? Is not the ideal golden age one in which all men are of one opinion, and what greater peace could we convey upon men than to cause them all to embrace one belief? If they would all believe as we do, they would be happy and bless us as their redeemers."

Such fallacious arguments, full of sophistry, are often used by the followers of dogmatic theology. If all men could be supplied with an equal share of wisdom, they would all be equally happy; but opinion is not knowledge, ignorance is not wisdom, animal comfort is not the object of life, knowledge of external things is not the aim of existence, a merely imaginary salvation does not convey immortality. If all men could be transformed into stones, all would cease to suffer; if they were all enclosed in one common tomb, they would all be equally at peace.

The object of life is not life itself, but the attainment of a higher degree of perfection in the ladder of evolution; the attainment of a higher state of consciousness, which can be reached only through that spiritual knowledge which ennobles the soul.\ What would a being transferred into the spiritual realm do, if it possessed merely a knowledge of externals, but no consciousness for spiritual things, and consequently no power to perceive its surroundings? What would it do in the realm of Divine Wisdom, if it merely possessed the artificial light of Logic, but not the light of the living *Christ?* Surrounded by darkness, it would exist within the hell created by its own imagination, until the laws of its being would permit it to come back again to this earth, to seek for light in a new expression in form.

"Man has before him life and death; whatever he chooses will be given to him."[1] If he chooses to remain in darkness and ignorance, trusting that another will do his own work, his choice will be death in the spirit; if he wants to live he must work; for the truth, when it once enters the heart, will bring peace to the spirit; but to the soul it will bring the *sword* with which to combat selfish desires and to conquer Self.[2]

It is not "Morals" that we attempt to preach, but the awakening of the inner man to a realization of his own true manhood. It is not a scheme of salvation by which divine justice may be cheated, or a certain rule of conduct that we wish to establish, but the attainment of *knowledge.* The external conduct of a man, however good it may be, amounts to little as far as he himself is concerned, unless it is a true expression of the internal

---

[1] John iii. 13.   [2] Sirach xv. 17.

state of his mind. (Good conduct accompanied with evil thoughts and desires is often a result of cowardice and hypocrisy.)

As the evening approached, Jehoshua, with his disciples, retired to the house of a friend, to partake of the supper that had been prepared for them. He spoke to them of the immortality of that divine and universal essence contained in every soul, and how all souls in which this principle would become self-conscious, would thereby be rendered consciously immortal. He spoke of that divine life of Intelligence that renders the soul which it permeates luminous, like a ray of sunlight pervading a crystal globe, while the souls of those who were filled only with the love of self become dark, when the mortal intellect whose illusive light illuminated them during terrestrial life had become dissolved.

"He who clings to his lower self," he said, "will die with the latter; but he who, even during his life upon this earth, rises above all selfish thoughts, and becomes conscious of being an integral part of the divine Spirit that pervades all creation, will live. The soul of Man, having during his terrestrial life become united with God, when the physical body dies, returns with the spirit to the divine *Centre* to which it is attracted by the laws of its constitution, and will bring its own light with it, thereby increasing the light of that Centre. Thus it will glorify God, and an increased radiance of Light will take place and bless the hearts of mankind.[1] Partake ye all

---

[1] John xxiv. 17.

of that Light which gives life, for it is the nourishment of the soul, it will form the substance of the celestial body;[1] but the wine of spiritual love is the great fiery stimulus, that causes the souls of men to expand beyond the narrow spheres of self-adulation and personal existence, so that they may become like gods. There is no one to condemn you for your mistakes, unless you condemn yourself. Those who are unable to see the truth, will not be punished for their ignorance; but they will remain in darkness until they learn to open their eyes and to see the light; but those who are conscious of the truth and reject it, prefer death to life, and they therefore commit spiritual suicide, that unpardonable sin, which causes their own destruction."[2]

They complained to him how difficult it was to keep the thoughts continually directed towards the Eternal and to exclude selfish desires, and he told them that in proportion as they would love all mankind they would forget their love of self, and that as their thoughts would reach up towards the Infinite, their own spheres of consciousness would expand beyond the region of selfish desires. Moreover, he taught them a prayer, which he had learned in Egypt from the book of "*Kadish*," and which they might repeat in silence, keeping their thoughts fastened to the sentiments therein, to prevent them from sinking into the lower region of minds. In its esoteric meaning it may be rendered as follows:—

[1] Matthew xxv. 26. [2] John xii. 47.

"Let us glorify the universal Spirit of Divine Wisdom, from whose Light the consciousness of all beings originates; let us worship Him by sacrificing to Him all thoughts of self and all individual self-interests, and by rising up to His sphere in our thoughts and aspirations. May no earthly wish ever cause us to act against the universal Will of the Supreme, who rules all things in the visible and invisible universe by His unchangeable Law! May his power cause all mankind to grow in daily knowledge and to expand in Love, and may all men awaken to a realization of their true state as spiritual powers, temporarily connected with mortal forms! Let no thoughts of our past deeds, when we were in a state of darkness, mar our present state of supreme happiness, and let us forget all the evils that have ever been inflicted upon us by others. Let us strive to become free from all the attractions of matter and sensuality, and submerging our consciousness into that of the Universal and Supreme, become redeemed from the illusion of self, the source of all evil; for the mortal self of man is merely an unsubstantial shadow, while the Real and Substantial is the Indivisible, Eternal, and Infinite Spirit."

While discussing such matters, the evening passed away and the sun sank down below the western horizon, when they arose to take a walk in the suburbs, to breathe the balmy air of spring and to pass the night in the garden of *Gethsemane*.

As long as the soul of man is chained to its material

form, there will always be moments when that which is mortal in man attempts to assert its claims. The love of life is an inherent property of the animal element in nature, and the mortal parts in the constitution of Jehoshua seemed to feel the impending doom and revolted. He therefore left his disciples and went a *little higher up* on the hill, to seek consolation from the Divinity in his soul and to gather courage and strength, and while he sunk his thoughts down to the utmost depths of his soul and seriously prayed to the Godhead within, he became lost to all his surroundings. Again that divine Light which at the time of his Initiation and upon the Mount of Transfiguration had filled his soul, illumined his mind, filling him with consolation and joy, so that he forgot that he was an isolated being and realized his Unity with the Eternal Father of All.

THE FINAL INITIATION.

The light of Divine Wisdom will not be seen in its purity until the clouds of matter that obscure the sight are dispersed; the sanctuary of the temple cannot be seen until the curtain is lifted.

THE light of torches appeared in the distance, the clang of arms resounded through the garden of Gethsemane, and the guardians of the temple accompanied by a crowd of fanatical Jews approached the grove where Jehoshua was absorbed in deep meditation while his disciples slept. The approach of the soldiers called him roughly back from the realities of the Ideal to the illusions of Earth, and the disciples fled in dismay; nor would the guard have permitted them to escape if they had remained; still less would they have suffered them to offer any resistance. They knew Jehoshua very well, for they had seen him many times in the temple; but the Truth they did not know face to face; they only knew it from hearsay and from the revelations made by Logic, the traitor.

They bound him and took him through the now almost deserted streets to the house of the High Priest, where he was kept a prisoner until the day began to dawn, and then they led him out of the city upon a hill and threw stones at him until he was dead, according to their law.

Thus the body of Jehoshua Ben-Pandira died; and as his great soul left its earthly tenement, the latter grew dark, having been deserted by the light of the spirit, and its tombs opened to let the vital powers escape; the veil of Matter, which during his terrestrial life had hidden the sanctuary of the Temple of the Universal Spirit from the sight of his soul, was now rent asunder, and the genius of Jehoshua went rejoicing back to the bosom of his eternal Father, to receive his final Initiation into that Mystery which can be known only to those who have attained a state beyond all imaginable isolated existence, but which consists in becoming *one* with that which really *is* and in partaking of its divine nature and universal self-consciousness. As his great Soul became resurrected from the grave of Matter, wherein it had been imprisoned during its terrestrial life, all the intellectual powers of his mind arose from their prisons and walked again in the bright daylight of Divine Wisdom.

After he had expired, they nailed his body upon a wooden cross and left it there exposed, as a warning to all who might henceforth dare to defend the truth against superstition and scepticism, and the hate with which they regarded him has descended upon their successors, so that even now, when the latter refer to *Jehoshua Ben-Pandira*, they speak of him merely as the man whose name ought not to be uttered.

His followers took the corpse down from the cross and buried it secretly, so that it should be no more desecrated, for they looked upon their Master with great reverence and almost worshipped him as a god. In fact, the belief that the *person* of Jehoshua had actually been a god gained more and more credence among the ignorant, and there was especially one man, named *Peter*, who, having been an ignorant fisherman, had become one of the disciples of Jehoshua, whose teachings he could not comprehend, and who now began to teach this erroneous doctrine. He was seriously opposed by *Paul*, a man of superior understanding, who taught that the universal God could not be a mortal man; but that He was eternal and omnipresent; that "He is before all things and by Him all things exist";[1] and that *the Christ* is likewise an eternal, omnipresent principle, the first born and greatest of all spiritual Powers, constituting Himself the head of that universal spiritual Temple, wherein the Spirit of Divine Wisdom in his fulness dwells, and which not merely embraces all mankind,[2] but the whole of the Universe with all its inhabited worlds; that "church" whose High Priest is the Truth, whose dogma is universal fraternal Love, and whose knowledge comes to all who open their hearts to receive it.[3]

But *Peter*, whose spiritual perception had never been opened like that of *Paul*, and who was, moreover, a vain and ambitious person, wanting to rule and to occupy himself, the place of Jehoshua, taught that men could not be saved by the attainment of Divine Wisdom, but

---

[1] Colossians i. 17.   [2] *Ibid.* iii. 11.   [3] *Ibid.* i. 27.

only through the authority of the church ; and as there are always more people willing to take the easy road and submit to be saved by somebody, than such as are willing to use strong efforts for themselves, the doctrines of Peter found more adherents than those of Jehoshua and Paul, and thus Peter, by teaching a doctrine contrary to that of Jehoshua, became a traitor to his Master and denied him thrice even before the cock had crowed to announce the dawn of a new day of enlightenment to mankind. Thus the darkness of ignorance was re-established upon the Earth, and the sacrifice of Jehoshua was, to a great extent rendered useless by those who claimed to be his successors.

But the God that gave Jehoshua life and spoke through his lips is not dead. He still enters the heart without asking permission of the Pharisees and the Scribes. If his presence is once realized within the soul, then will man begin to know the *King of the Jews*, and bow down before Him. Then will the moneychangers, the sophists, and scribes be driven away. The three *Sages from the East*, the principal powers of Man, his *Will*, *Thought*, and *Action*, guided by the *star* of Wisdom, will come and offer a continual sacrifice to the new-born God ; the soul of Man will become transformed from a stable into a temple, wherein *Herodes*, the king of selfishness, has no jurisdiction. The Christ growing strong within man will select those of his intellectual powers which are suitable to become His *disciples;* he will cure man's mental blindness, purify his mind of its leprosy, drive out the evil spirits of envy, malice, and lust from the soul, and make the virtues which have died, alive again, even if they have already begun to acquire a bad odor. New powers will awaken within, but their development involves the crucifixion and death of all that is evil and selfish in Man. Then when selfishness has died and been buried, will the free spirit within resurrect from its tomb, and its glorified form will become visible to the eyes of the soul.

Listen! A well-known voice, which no one can misunderstand, is calling within your heart. It is the true Saviour, speaking now as he did when he spoke in the heart of Jehoshua: "I am the Way, the Truth, and the Life; no one cometh unto the Father but by me." This Christ has never died, but men have spiritually died when they became unconscious of his existence. He has been always with you, but you did not know it; because your attention was attracted to your semi-animal self. He is your own God, the divine self of all men. He lives in that sphere where no separation and isolation exists; but where all are as one. He requires no substitute to speak to your heart, no deputy to enter into communication with you, no "successor," for He is here Himself. He is yourself, and you will be He if you will merely open your eyes and become conscious of his Divinity within yourself by living in accordance with his divine Will.

Not to depend upon the promises of another man, even if they are said to emanate from a god; but to exert your own efforts and to put your trust in that which is divine within yourself; to become conscious of the existence of God by rising up to the highest regions of thought and to remain therein; this will be the religion of the future — the only religion worthy of an enlightened humanity. Then will the true faith be restored; the Scribes and Pharisees, priestcraft, superstition and scepticism will disappear, and our works will correspond with our thoughts. Then will our knowledge not be based upon the opinion of any other man, but upon our own power to see and perceive the truth, and upon an understanding of the laws of Nature and the corresponding nature of Man.

As long as men crucify the truth, and keep it hanging between superstition and doubt, the two thieves that steal the reason of man away, they will not be able to become self-conscious of its divinity. To obtain self-knowledge of the Truth, man must be one with it, and exalt it by exalting himself above the sphere of credulity into the region of pure spiritual knowledge. Eternal Truth is immortal, and cannot be grasped by mortal man; it can only be known to that principle which is immortal in man. The Truth can be known only to itself.

THE CHURCH.

Woe to him who pretends to be a co-operator of God without being a god. Let those who desire to reform the world begin by reforming themselves.

Soon after the death of Jehoshua a spook is said to have appeared to Peter and his associates, and assuming the shape of Jehoshua, to have said to those present: "*Whosoever sins ye remit, they are remitted to him; and whosoever sins ye retain, they are retained.*" Whether this self-evident falsehood, contrary to all the doctrines of Christ, was uttered by an *Elemental*, parading in the *astral remnant* of Jehoshua, or whether it was — like many other sayings contained in the Bible — a pious interpolation, made in the interest of the church, or whether it has an esoteric meaning, referring — not to the "apostles," but to the *memory* of Man; — the acceptation of this doctrine completely neutralized all that Jehoshua ever taught; it caused divine wisdom, justice, and truth to be henceforth regarded as matters of little importance; it did away with the eternal God of the universe, and established in its place the rule of a man-made church.

Absurd and monstrous as such a doctrine will necessarily appear to all who are able to use the power of enlightened reason with which they have been endowed by God, it was nevertheless greedily grasped by the ignorant and by those who worshipped at the altar of Self; for in the place of the invisible and intangible God of Humanity, whose presence can only be perceived spiritually by those who are pure in their hearts, and whose eternal laws cannot be changed by men, it furnished them with visible and tangible gods in human shapes, who could be bribed and bargained with; with a church that had the power to permit mankind to sin, and nevertheless to admit them to heaven after their death.

The words spoken by Jehoshua, when he said: "Come unto me, all who are suffering sorrow, and I will give you peace. Follow me; my yoke is easy and my burden is light," were now travestied by the rulers of the church, and misapplied by interpreting them in an external sense, entirely opposed to that which Jehoshua intended to convey; for he meant to say that those who would open their hearts to Divine Wisdom and follow the dictates of the Truth, would easily rise above the sufferings caused by the illusions of self; while the false prophets made it appear, as if those who would join their church and submit to their rules, would be saved from the labor which the acquisition of self-knowledge entails. In vain the apostle Paul denounced such an erroneous doctrine and said that he was preaching not a belief in a *person*, but a *faith* in the universal power of *Christ*,[1] and that those who preached any other Christ but the *Logos* were teaching errors and belonged

[1] Galatians i. 12, 16.

to the powers of darkness : his doctrine, like that of Jehoshua, was comprehended by few. He was denounced by Peter as being a visionary, and even his epistles were forged and falsified for the purpose of deluding the seekers after the truth.[1]

Thus while the true and eternal, invisible and spiritual church of *The Christ* is based upon the Truth, the visible sectarian "Christian" churches upon this globe are based upon a falsehood; and while the former will exist eternally, the latter will exist as long as the powers of evil prevail.

The doctrine of a personal extracosmic deity who can be bribed with sacrifices, was too much engrafted into the minds of the Jews to be easily eradicated by the teachings of Jehoshua and Paul; and when soon afterwards great misfortunes befell that nation, they were still more in need of a saviour to accomplish a work which they were too indolent to accomplish themselves. Jehovah did not fulfil his promises, and the claims of the newly made Christian god were taken into consideration.

"What shall we do to be saved?" asked the poor and oppressed; and the glad response was, "Join the church of the Nazarenes; and even if you fail to obtain any relief during terrestrial life, you will obtain untold pleasures in heaven."

"But what must we do," they asked, "to obtain such a heaven?"—"Nothing at all," was the answer, "but allow yourself to be baptized with water and believe

[1] G. Massey, "Paul the Gnostic Opponent of Peter."

THE CHURCH. 189

that God will save you through the power of the church; for he has resigned his authority and authorized the priests to bind or to loose: he has intrusted them with the keys to heaven and hell, and if you follow the dictates of those people whom God has appointed to rule in his place, you may believe yourself to be free of all danger."

Such an advice was easy enough to follow. The sect of the Nazarenes grew; and as the number of its agnostic members increased, its gnostic members disappeared from sight; superstition took the place of knowledge, mere opinions the place of the true faith. The ancient doctrines of the sages contained in the books of Hermes, and the prophets which had heretofore been guarded with jealous care from the eyes of the ignorant, became the common property of those who were unable to understand their meaning; they misinterpreted them in various ways, divisions of opinions took place, and sects arose like mushrooms after a rainy night, and the desecration of the sacred mysteries soon began to claim its penalty in rivers of blood.

To the huts of the poor and into the palaces of the rich penetrated the gospel of joy and salvation made easy. The religious systems of the Romans were decaying rapidly, because they, too, had lost the keys of their mysteries, and the divine and intelligent powers pervading the Universal Mind, which had been allegorically represented by their deities, had begun to be looked upon as being the personal gods and goddesses, whom their images represented. The people believed their own religious opinions to be threatened by the new sect, and persecutions began. These persecutions merely served to strengthen the Christians and to give rise to a heroism almost unparalleled in history.

The arenas in Rome resounded with the cries of the martyrs; Nubian tigers and African lions were fed with living men and women, and the bodies of the Christians, enveloped in combustible substances and set on fire, served as living torches for the orgies of an insane emperor; but for every victim that died, hundreds of new converts joined the ranks. While the original gnostic Christians had attained eternal life by that *mystic death*, by which the lower self becomes as it were dead to all attractions of matter, while the spirit rises above the plane of self, the new converts, misunderstanding that doctrine, imagined to gain heaven by sacrificing their physical forms. To die "for the sake of Christ" and for the benefit of the church was considered a privilege, followed by an eternal reward, and thousands rushed voluntarily into the jaws of death; thus imitating the Indian religious fanatics, who, likewise in consequence of a similar misunderstanding, threw themselves down before the car of the *Juggernath*, to be crushed by its wheels, and to bargain away a short life upon this earth for an eternal enjoyment in heaven.[1]

---

[1] The doctrine of the Hindus is, that he who succeeds in seeing the *Dwarf* hidden within the *Car of the Juggernath*, will attain eternal life. The "Dwarf" means the spiritual principle in the soul of man, and the

The church grew, being continually watered by rivers of blood, and it became a power, rivalling the power of the governments. Kings and emperors watched its growth with jealous eyes; and as they saw that they could not suppress it, they asked: "What shall we do to make this power useful to us?" and the church replied: "Lend us the power of your arm, by which you enslave the bodies of men, and we will lend you the power by which we enslave their minds." They accepted the offer, and made the pact with the church, and the Evil One, whose offer Jehoshua had rejected while in the wilderness, signed the contract, putting the name of "Christ" to the document.

The Christians ceased to be persecuted, and the church now became a persecutor in the name of Christ, being assisted in her work by the powers of the state. Europe was at that time overrun with idlers and vagabonds, and the "Holy Land" in the East, which they could not find in their souls, looked inviting for pillage and plunder. Religious fanatics inflamed the populace, and soon Europe emptied its dregs upon the "heathen," and murder and rape were committed in

---

"Car" is the body, and it is perfectly true that those who learn to know the Divinity in their souls, while living in the body, thereby attain spiritual consciousness. But the ignorant, misunderstanding this doctrine, applied it in a literal sense. They had a wagon constructed, and called it the Juggernath, and as it was drawn through the streets, they crowded around it, to see a dwarf, whom they believed to be hidden therein. Many were crushed by the wheels in their vain attempts to see that dwarf, and as such a death was said to be meritorious, and to open the portals of heaven, it became gradually fashionable to commit suicide in this manner.

the name of Him who taught the religion of universal fraternal love to humanity.

The God of the Christian church was as impotent as that of the Jews. He had no power to save his worshippers from the fate they deserved; but as he grew in size he increased the fanaticism and the greed of his priests. The "holy inquisition" was inaugurated, and fagots kindled by well-fed monks depopulated the country and filled the treasury of the church. Millions of human beings expired upon the rack or stake, in dungeons or upon the battle-field, and the most horrible crimes were committed by the God of the church that paraded in the mask of Christ.

At last a reaction began, for the age had become ripe for a change. The spirit of Luther overthrew the monster at Rome; but while he succeeded to a certain extent in driving back the powers of darkness that ruled the country, he could not remove the clouds that prevent mankind from seeing the light. By the side of the gloomy cathedrals of Rome, he erected churches, whose windows admitted more light; but when he entered therein, an army of devils followed him. His temples are built upon the same foundation as that of the church of Rome; namely, upon a belief in salvation by external means of that perishing thing called the personal self. Both churches, with all their subdivisions, are based upon the selfish propensities inherent in the semi-animal nature in man; both appeal to his selfish desire for reward and to his fear of punishment in the problematical hereafter. Both are resting upon the erroneous belief that Divine authority can be conferred upon man-ordained priests by a man-made church; but while the *Roman* church — if once the fundamental falsehood upon which she bases her claims is accepted — may appeal to Logic, the most powerful devil in man, to prove her other pretensions, the claims of the Protestant church for Divine authority to save mankind are not so supported.

What is that thing which these people desire to save, whose existence they desire to preserve, whose life they crave to prolong? What is this personal self? It has no self-existence and possesses no life of its own. It is a continually changing conglomeration of principles, endowed with a continually changing consciousness. If it were not for the power of memory, which connects these continually changing states of mind with each other, and which is itself subject to change, no man would ever know that he is the same person he was an hour ago. The only thing in man which is not subject to change is his consciousness of the Eternal, and whenever he enters that state, he forgets that he is a person, becomes unconscious of the isolation of form, and is only conscious of being in the Infinite Spirit. These are facts, which require no arguments for proof, but which every one may know by reflection and self-examination: they are self-evident. But this consciousness of the eternal needs no salvation; it is already safe, for it is the consciousness of the

Christ; the only state in which man can be immortal, because it is not subject to change. ⟨Salvation is therefore an internal process which no man can produce for another, but which each one must accomplish within himself.⟩ To enter that state of consciousness in the Eternal is the only possible salvation for man.

As long as men possess no self-knowledge, they will clamor for a belief; as long as they possess insufficient self-control, they will crave to be the slaves of a master; and priestcraft, assuming the garb of Religion, takes her harp and sings the sweet lullaby: —

"Come to me, all of ye who are troubled with sorrow; I will take the load from your shoulders. I will save you the trouble of thinking and of mastering your passions. I will make the battle for self-control easy for you by thinking for you and assuming control over you. I will take care of your thoughts while you live; I will give you bladders to swim and crutches to walk with, and you will rest warm on my maternal bosom. I will lull you to sleep when you die, and take care of you after your death."

Thus the siren song is heard, while the ship glides along upon the storm-tossed waves of the river of life, and the helmsman listens, and dropping the oar he falls in a drowsy sleep and indulges in fanciful dreams, trusting the guidance of the ship to a form without substance or power, until it founders upon the rocks.

⟨Great is the imaginary power by which men are deluded, and which is called the authority of the church.

It has become a dangerous rival of the governments, and the day may arrive when the latter will curse the day when they signed the compact.

The unreality of the pretensions of the modern church has come to the understanding of the more enlightened masses. They have begun to laugh at her claims, but the church laughs at them. She clings for protection to the skirts of the goddess of fashion; the goddess gives her bright ornaments of brass and glittering tinsel; she furnishes her with pomp and elaborate ceremonies, and men are used to imagine that they are in need of these things: they borrow them from the church, and the latter again takes hold of the leading-strings.

And while this farce is played, the true church of the *Christ* is deserted. Clear and strong shines the bright sunshine of Divine Wisdom through the transparent roof of its dome, as it did in ancient times; but the crowds of worshippers that used to crowd the halls have deserted the temple. The sacrificial fires upon the altars have gone out for want of fuel; for those who used to worship in the temple of Wisdom now worship at the altar of Self. The temple of Truth, wherein all humanity unknowingly live and whose altars exist in the innermost centre of every human heart, is the temple, where the divine Redeemer still continues to teach, in spite of all the Pharisees and scribes by which he is now surrounded. External churches decay, unless they are upheld and supported by man; but this eternal temple needs no support from mortals: it will never cease to exist. It asks for no favors and fees; but the condition to be admitted to it is an entire renunciation of self. It requires no one to explain its doctrines, for the truth becomes clear to all as soon as they become able to see it, and all will recognize it by its beauty as soon as they draw the veil from its face. The foundation of that temple is knowledge, — not that illusive knowledge taught by mortal man, which refers merely to the illusions of sense, but that spiritual knowledge which arises from a realization of the truth. Fear and doubt do not enter that temple, nor is there any difference of opinion; because the truth is only one in *the absolute*, and all who know it have the same knowledge. There are no inducements held out in that temple to cause men to be virtuous but the beauty of virtue; there is no other penalty for the wicked but that which naturally follows the disobedience of the law. There is only one supreme Law, the Love of absolute Good. When men become satiated with the worship of self and of living on salt sea fruit, they will again return to the Temple of Wisdom to partake of the water of Truth.

CONCLUSION.

There can be no higher wisdom than a realization of Divine Truth.

IN the preceding pages we have attempted to draw a picture of Jehoshua Ben-Pandira, in whom the eternal Christ became manifest, for the purpose of bringing the mind nearer to an intellectual understanding of the real nature of Man, and the soul nearer to a realization of the presence of the real, living, eternal, and only true Christ, the Spirit of Divine Wisdom, that may become manifest in all who are receptive for it.

Many of the doctrines we have attempted to explain are not new. They are taught in Christian pulpits, and moreover they are also taught — but in different forms — in the pulpits of those whom the Christians are pleased to call the "heathen." It will therefore be readily seen by the unprejudiced observer, that — while denouncing the abuses made of religion by priestcraft — neither Jehoshua nor ourselves have been attempting to overthrow the truth of Christianity, nor of any other religious system. We have attempted to show that, while the Christ whom the Christian sects are preaching is merely a human being, whose work of redemption is a thing of the past, the Christ taught by the spiritual perception of Man is an eternal, ever-present, infinite Power, whose work of redemption is still and continually going on within the hearts of all who worship the truth.

It may be left to those who are able to think, to decide for themselves, whether or not a belief in the existence of an historical personal Christ is compatible with their own intuition and necessary, sufficient, or useful for their salvation; but whether such a belief is justified by facts, or merely insisted upon as a necessity for those who are not yet able to grasp the deeper mysteries of religion, it seems self-evident that if such an historical belief is made the main pillar of the Christian faith, and if Christians are satisfied with such an external belief, they will not gain any real knowledge of the truth; for he who rests satisfied with an adopted creed or opinion will seek no further, and remaining idle, his progress will come to a stop.

We have attempted to show that the events so beautifully described in the Bible are allegories, representing occurrences which have not only taken place in the past, but which are continually taking place within the psychic organization of man, and which will continue to occur in the future; for God, Nature, and Man are one undivided whole; the processes going on within the Universal Mind are continually mirrored forth within the mind of man, and the internally acting powers of Universal Nature find their expression in external forms, as the thoughts of man find their external expression in his physical form and in his external actions.

Whether a belief in an "historical" Christ walking upon the earth in the shape of a man is justifiable or not, it can only be useful to induce mankind to look up to him as an ideal whose example they may imitate. To enable us to live up to a high ideal, it is not necessary that the latter should have been incorporated in a gross material form: it is far more necessary that our ideal should take form within ourselves.

It is one of the fundamental doctrines of occult science, that man is the product of his own thoughts; he is that which he makes himself by the way he thinks and acts, for his external form is nothing else but an outward symbol of his internal character, modified by the want of plasticity of the gross matter composing his body, for gross matter is not sufficiently plastic to change in form as rapidly as his thoughts. The matter composing the soul is more plastic. If our thoughts are continually low and vulgar, it will become correspondingly degraded; but if we are continually thinking of a high Ideal, our Ideal will take form within ourselves. If we are satisfied with a belief in an historical Christ without seeking to cause or enable a Christ to grow within ourselves, such a belief will not be merely useless, but it will be an impediment in our way to perfection.

The object of true religion is to ennoble mankind and to awaken men to a realization of the divinity of the Spirit within themselves. Religion in its *theoretical* aspect means a real knowledge of the relations which exist between man and the eternal Source from which his Spirit emanated in the beginning; religion in its *practical* aspect means the union of man with God, — a union that cannot be effected through the external interference or permission of a clergyman, but which must be effected by the power of the internal Will. There is no real knowledge to be attained by merely learning a theory; there is no real knowledge unless the theory is confirmed by practice.

We would not abolish the external forms of religious worship, because forms are necessary for those who live in a form to lead them up to higher conceptions of the truth by means of an idealization of forms, until they arrive at a state in which they may realize the existence of that which is above form and above expression in language; but if the practice of a religion is not at all in accordance with its theory; if the form is made to assume the prerogatives of the living spirit; if a knowledge of the truth is made to rest upon a belief in an improbable tale of an external historical event, while the truth itself is denied admittance; if religion, instead of being used to ennoble mankind, is made to serve the temporal purposes of the churches; then will the living spirit depart from the forms, and the forms themselves will decay.

Such a decay is almost universally observed. Even those who cling to the church must be aware of the fact that in visiting the churches they receive nothing but what they bring with them to the church, and that a sermon is only effective upon the audience if it gives expression to the sentiments of the latter; but the masses of the people are beginning to look upon the promises made by the churches as being drafts upon a bank which does not exist, and upon the "places of worship" as serving rather for houses of fashionable resort and religious amusement, than as places where anything useful is taught. They instinctively feel that there can be no salvation by merely external means, and having been misled by the superficial arguments of our modern beer-house philosophers and inoculated with the poison of scepticism, they have begun to doubt the possibility of a life after the death of the body, and therefore they make no efforts to save themselves and to develop that internal power by which they might become conscious of a higher state of existence.

They have come to regard life as being its own object and to ridicule the idea of any conscious existence after the death of the mortal form. They look upon material comforts as being of supreme importance to man and the only means for the attainment of happiness. New luxuries are invented every day, and they become to-morrow indispensable necessities for existence; but still there is no contentment. The gratification of desires merely begets new desires as long as the power to enjoy that gratification exists, and thus the chains which bind man to matter are growing stronger day by day, while the claims of the imprisoned spirit are laughed at and neglected. Christ, being looked upon as being merely an historical person, a thing of the past, is sent away to the garret, and that higher state of consciousness which constitutes the true Christ in Man is a thing equally unknown to the layman as it is to the priest.

The world swarms with reformers. They are shaking the foundations of the Church and the State, and the temples are tottering; they resemble a swarm of birds flying around a tree, seeking to change the nature of the tree by picking at the leaves; they seek to trim the branches, while they have no means of changing the nature of the sap, and therefore their efforts are of little avail; they can merely produce ruin, but they cannot build up. Men have become unnatural and crave for unnatural things; external life, instead of being a true expression of the internal thought-life, is entirely out of harmony with the latter; words are no more the expression of thoughts, and acts are not in harmony with the words.

It seems that the only way to restore mankind to its natural condition is to assist it to rise up to a realization of the truth; not to establish a new religious system, based upon some new theory, but a religion based upon self-knowledge and knowledge of self. To do this, we need not present humanity with some new dogma, but we may submit to them some thoughts for their own consideration.

According to the Wisdom-Religion of the ancients, aboriginal Man was a spiritual power, emanating from the Great First Cause of all existence, descending gradually into Matter, and becoming more and more material during that descent, which lasted for millions of ages, until he became differentiated in corporeal and gross material forms of two different sexes. His incorruptible spiritual principle, the foundation of his existence, became, so to say, concentrated within the innermost centre of his being and veiled by matter of a corruptible kind. In consequence of this "Fall," his communication with the world of *Light* was cut off, his "inner eye" closed to the perception of things of the spirit, while his external senses developed for the perception of corporeal and external things. From this state of degradation no mortal man can save himself, nor would any man ever make the attempt to rise again to his former state of spirituality, not knowing that such a state exists or is possible to attain; if it were not for that divine Light of the *Logos*, called *the Christ*, continually acting through the veil of Matter upon the spark of Divinity still existing within the soul of man and stimulating the same into activity through the powers of Intuition and Conscience, attempting to induce Man to seek for that higher state of which mortal man does not know, but of which the *Soul* feels, the existence. If man conquers the living elements acting within his material nature, and which are appealing to his love for animal life and animal pleasure; and if he follows the voice of Wisdom within, the gross elements of his "Soul" become gradually refined; the veil of Matter, which hides the spiritual world from his sight, becomes thinner, and at last he may arrive at a state in which he "dies" to the attractions of sense and is *reborn* in the spirit. This freedom from the attraction of Matter is that liberty for which man ought to strive; it is symbolized by the *Eagle* rising above the clouds of matter and enjoying the light of the Spirit. The true building of the Temple of Sol-Om-On consists, therefore, in the tearing down of the miserable hut built up of erroneous opinions and perverted tastes, — a hovel which we have erected ourselves by our own thoughts, and wherein we dwell. It consists in the opening of its walls and roof, so that the Light of the Truth may enter and drive away the darkness of its interior; it consists in the regaining of the power of the Spirit over Matter, — a power which is the natural birthright of immortal Man.

There are three stages by which this herculean task is accomplished and spiritual knowledge attained. The first is known to all men. It consists of the power to intuitively know the good from the bad, the just from the unjust, the pure from the impure, etc.; it is called "Conscience," or, more properly, spiritual *Inspiration*. The second degree of receptivity consists in the capacity, not only to feel, but to understand intellectually, spiritual truths. It is a state known only to those who have attained it, and it is called interior *Illumination*. The third degree is only attained by few, and the great majority of mankind in the West do not believe that it exists. It consists in an entire opening of the spiritual senses, by which spiritual realities become objectively perceptible to the soul of man, and it is called divine *Contemplation*. It is the highest kind of worship and true adoration.

These three modes of perception are as natural and as easily comprehended by those who know by experience the higher nature of Man, as are the sensual perceptive powers of man's semi-animal body to those who have studied his perishable form; but to those who know nothing about the higher nature of man and who do not believe in his spiritual powers, anything higher than the semi-animal existence of man is incomprehensible and incredible, and man's spiritual powers do not exist *for them*.

There have, however, even in the most ancient times, up to the present day, existed men in whom this power of divine contemplation has been developed, and who are therefore in possession of superior knowledge, and if we desire to receive information in regard to spiritual things before we have attained the power to perceive them ourselves, we may look to those men for instruction. Not that a belief in their doctrines should be the final end of our aspirations for knowledge; but as a traveller who has gone through a wilderness may indicate the way to those who follow after him, so may the teachings of the *Adepts* serve as landmarks and guides to those who wander about in search of the truth. Such a man was Jehoshua the Adept.

Such men are not easily to be found within the churches of to-day; for ever since the representatives of the churches have lost the key to the understanding of the mysteries of religion, and begun to mistake the forms for the spirit, churchianism has become identical with narrow-mindedness and dogmatism. They cling to beliefs accepted from each other; while true Knowledge is free of foreign opinions and lives in her own realization of the truth.

The attainment of this knowledge is that glorious resurrection from the darkness of ignorance, by which the Spirit of Man, bursting the shell of matter, arises from the tomb in which he was imprisoned and regains his previous freedom. It is not a state to be expected in the problematical hereafter, when the physical body has returned to its elements; for death of the body can merely relieve us of things which have become useless to us: it cannot give us anything which we do not possess when we die. The object of man's life is to rise up higher in the scale of evolution, while he is living upon this earth; to develop new powers during his contact with matter; to acquire more strength and knowledge during his terrestrial existence, and on account of the latter; so that he may live in a higher state of consciousness and enjoy the possession of knowledge of spiritual truths, which he has acquired during his earthly career, unimpeded by the sensations arising from the sphere of illusions, when he re-enters the subjective state, the state of rest.

All the boasted knowledge of the science learned in schools contains no *real* knowledge whatever. It knows nothing of *absolute truth*. It is merely *relative* knowledge, and refers to the relations which external objects bear to each other; and all this knowledge, however useful it may be as long as we live in this world of external illusions and "objective hallucinations," will be entirely useless to us when we enter that state in which those illusions do not exist. The only true science, which is really useful to us in time and eternity, in our present condition, not less than in the hereafter, is the practical knowledge of the *Regeneration of Man.*

This knowledge is acquired neither by the study of theology and philosophy, nor by moralizing. It does not depend on any theoretical information in regard to terrestrial or celestial things, nor can spiritual regeneration be attained by leading a virtuous life for fear of the consequences that are likely to follow if we indulge in evil; it can only be acquired by a realization of the truth within our own selves. There is nothing to prevent any man from arriving at such a realization, except the lower tendencies of his mortal nature. The process of spiritual regeneration therefore involves a continual battle with this lower self; an unceasing fight between spiritual aspirations and earthly desires, in which the Spirit must gain the victory over Matter.

Spirit is Substance, Reality, Unity. It is therefore indestructible, indivisible, impenetrable, incorruptible, eternal. *Matter is an Aggregate, Multiplicity, Illusion;* it is therefore unsubstantial, divisible, corruptible, and subject to continual change. If man gains complete mastery over the "Matter" composing his own constitution, then will the realm of spiritual knowledge open before him, and he will become conscious of the presence of Christ. Then will the curtain that hides the sanctuary of the spiritual Temple of Divine Wisdom be rent asunder, the Great Mystery will be revealed, and Man will know his own saviour. Then will he arise from the tomb of Ignorance and walk again in the bright daylight of immortal Truth, that existed in the beginning and will exist at the end.

As long as man does not know his own divine self, he will continue to seek in externals that which can only be found interiorly; as long as he has not found his ideal in his own soul, he will cling to external ideals; but when he awakens to the realization of the divine power within himself, he will cease to look for salvation in external persons and things, and instead of seeking for a Christ in history he will find the true Jesus within himself.

www.ingramcontent.com/pod-product-compliance
Lightning Source LLC
Chambersburg PA
CBHW020905230426
43666CB00008B/1319